Tom

Best Wishes to the Crowley family
for continued success and prosperity.
We hope to continue building on a
solid foundation!   Grosk Kurz

George H. Kurz

THROUGH THE PORT OF PHILADELPHIA

Memoirs of Charles Kurz

1.   Portrait of Charles Kurz, 1939.

THROUGH THE PORT OF PHILADELPHIA

Memoirs of Charles Kurz

by
George H. Kurz, M.D.

DORRANCE & COMPANY, INCORPORATED
828 LANCASTER AVENUE • BRYN MAWR, PENNSYLVANIA 19010
Publishers Since 1920

CONTENTS

LIST OF ILLUSTRATIONS

2. Charles Kurz receiving American Merchant Marine Achievement Award
from Lyndon B. Johnson, July 12, 1963. From left: Commander Horan,
Senator Magnuson, Kurz, Vice President Johnson.

Preface

On May 22, 1963—Maritime Day—an announcement was made in New York that Charles Kurz of Philadelphia had been named Maritime Man of the Year for 1962 in recognition of his outstanding contributions to the American Merchant Marine. On July 12, just after his 75th birthday, Charles Kurz ascended the steps of the Capitol to receive that distinguished award from the Vice President of the United States.

On this crowning day in his life, Kurz was surrounded by family and friends, among them many government officials and luminaries of the shipping industry, including such dignitaries as Warren G. Magnuson, Chairman of the Senate Merchant Marine Committee; Thomas E. Staken, Chairman of the Federal Maritime Board; Donald W. Alexander, Chairman of the U. S. Maritime Administration: Alvin Shapiro, Vice President of the American Merchant Marine Institute; and Earle C. Clements, Consultant to the American Merchant Marine Institute and former U. S. Senator from Kentucky. Commanders Horan and McQuilling of the Robert L. Hague Post of the American Legion, which provided the trophy for the occasion, were also present.

Before this gathering of notables, Vice President Lyndon Baines Johnson, presenting the award in behalf of President John F. Kennedy, hailed Kurz's hard-earned reputation as a "first-class" and "above-board" ship operator. The award, he declared, should have been made long ago.

The trophy Charles Kurz received that day stood about two feet high, topped by the figure of a mermaid blowing into a conch shell, held in one hand like a trumpet, and holding a wreath in the other. Engraved on the central portion of the trophy were the words:

American Merchant Marine Achievement Award
of the
Robert L. Hague Merchant Marine Industries
Post No. 1242, American Legion
Department of New York

Embedded into the base were two rows of ship helms with space at the center of each for the name of an annual recipient. The impressive trophy remained in Charles Kurz's office for one year, and then he returned it to Washington to be passed on to the next recipient. But not until 1973 did he relinquish the day to day management of his business to become Chairman of the Board and not until 1984, after more than eight decades in shipping, did he become Chairman Emeritus.

The length of Charles Kurz's career reflects the determination and tenacity that were the richest legacies of his impoverished childhood. Born of poor German immigrant parents, Kurz had two serious strikes against him early in his life. The first was the death of his father when Charles was only two years old; the second, that in order to help support a family of five, Charles had to leave school before his thirteenth birthday and go out to work. In addition, he had to bear the burden of a cruel-hearted stepfather.

But even as a young man, Charles demonstrated unusual devotion to whatever work was his lot along with a remarkable ability to see the potential in whatever new opportunities arose. These characteristics won him the admiration and encouragement of several prominent and influential persons whose paths he crossed. From his job as clerk for a customs agent, Kurz eventually began his own business as a ship agent and custom house broker. Begun in 1914, that business continues today as Chas. Kurz Co. with offices at 115 Chestnut Street, Philadelphia, less than a block from the Custom House. Over the decades, Charles Kurz's career expanded to include operation of a fleet of tank ships that still sail around the world displaying the initials "C.K." as their insignia.

In spite of the humble and difficult circumstances of his youth, Charles Kurz rose to be a courageous business leader in Philadelphia, known for his unflagging determination to solve the toughest problems and his willingness to take the greatest risks. Where did he gain the know-how and courage to step out in spite of hardships and develop a business that would engage in worldwide commerce? Where did he find the inspiration and the vision to take bold new steps, to challenge the old ways of doing things, to dream of new possibilities? One part of the answer lies in the hardships themselves, for he met them as challenges to be overcome, and never yielded to discouragement. Another part of the answer lies in the relationships with certain special people who touched his life.

As the youngest of Charles Kurz's three sons, I came into his life when he was nearly forty-one years of age, already a highly successful businessman. I grew up as the son of a famous father. As a boy, I did not fully realize that all fathers were not similar to mine; in fact, only in recent years have I realized how unusual my own background was. Although I have no firsthand knowledge or recollection of my father's life prior to about 1935, when I was six years old, stories of his childhood, youth and early adult life in business began to fascinate me. I learned that his path in those early years had crossed that of several notable persons such as Russell Conwell, founder of Temple University; Chester W. Hill, the Collector of Customs for the Port of Philadelphia; Thomas Edison; William C. Sproul, Governor of Pennsylvania; and Charles S. Calwell, President of Corn Exchange National Bank. Some of these individuals had a profound influence on his life. They and others less famous, but no less important to him, gave him encouragement and inspiration.

But it is to my grandmother, a person whom I never knew, that I look as the one who most deeply influenced the life of her oldest son Charley. I have therefore devoted a considerable portion of this book to some of the remarkable incidents that I have heard my father recount about his mother. She managed to instill in him the unique ingenuity and business sense that stayed with him from the day he began as a twelve-year old errand boy in a custom house broker's office throughout his career.

Throughout his adult life Charles Kurz has been a source of leadership, strength and inspiration for his own family and for untold numbers of persons who have been associated with him in business.

More than a dozen years ago I urged my father to take the

stories that he told about his youth and early business experiences and make them into an autobiography. I was convinced that they provided some unusual insights into life in Philadelphia in the early years of the twentieth century. More importantly, the story of his own life can be an inspiration to aspiring youth three-fourths of a century later and conceivably for generations to come.

He did indeed make a start, dictating several chapters. But, although in his eighties at the time, he was still very active in the business. The press of work soon left those few chapters filed away at his office gathering dust along with various documents pertaining to the history of his business.

In early 1981 I realized that if these stories were ever to be assembled, it had better be now. My father was ninety-two and, though frail in body, his mind was alert and his memory incredibly clear both for recent events as well as for occurrences of the remote past. I began encouraging him to tell me the stories again, only to discover that there were many I had never heard before that were equally fascinating as the old ones. The pages that follow are a compilation of the reflections that I have been able to gather from his old files as well as the recent recounting of most of the incidents.

This volume does not provide either an exhaustive biography of Charles Kurz or a comprehensive history of the companies he founded. Instead, I have presented a series of episodes and anecdotes that illustrate a simple business principle, offer an explanation for a prejudice, demonstrate the building of character, or show the effect of encouragement from a mentor.

Born on June 25, 1888, Charles Kurz, now at ninety-six years of age, still resides in his native Philadelphia with his second wife, the former Anne T. Moran. His physical health has prevented him from going to his office for the past six years. Nevertheless, he has remained interested in the business and managed to keep informed of its activities and abreast of the whereabouts of the ships that bear his initials around the world.

—George Kurz
July 1984

Publisher's note: Charles Kurz died on February 2, 1985, shortly after this book was written. The text remains in its original form.

Part I

3. Charles's mother, Katharina Heck Kall, probably 1912. See Chapter 9 regarding Katharina's marriage to John Kall.

Chapter 1

BOYHOOD IN THE MARKET PLACE

When Katharina Heck Kurz's husband died in April 1891, at the age of thirty-three, she was left with two young daughters, Mary and Elizabeth, and one son, Charles, who was not quite three years old. A fourth child, Gus, was yet to be born.

Like Katharina, her husband Gottlob had been a German immigrant. The fourth of six children of a farmer from Talheim named Johannes Friedrich Kurz, Gottlob was the first member of his family to come to America. It was in 1880, eight years after his father's death, that Gottlob, then only twenty-two years old, arrived in Philadelphia. He was followed a year later by his older brother, Wilhelm, and two years later by a younger brother, Karl. Like Gottlob, Karl died at an early age, thirty-five, in Philadelphia. Wilhelm went to work on a farm and did very well; he and his wife eventually rented it for themselves.[1]

Katharina Heck, born in the farming village of Waldangelloch near Heidelberg, Germany, was preceded in America by an older brother, Christian Heck, who emigrated to avoid the army. Heck wrote home to say what a fine country America was and how well he was doing; he urged his sister to join him. Katharina got enough money together to pay her fare and finally came to Philadelphia, where she went to work as a cook in the home of the Bamberger family, owners of Bamberger's department store.

Gottlob and Katharina met in America and were married at the Salem German Reformed Church at 4th Street and Fairmount Avenue on April 28, 1883.

Gottlob Kurz, who was an expert cabinetmaker, was studying

---

[1]The farm extended from Bustleton Avenue along Cottman Avenue to Five Points and south to Magee Avenue.

to be a minister at the time of his death in 1891. And so Katharina found herself with sole responsibility for raising her children and no money with which to do so.

Somehow, however, she managed to cope with the hardships of life as a widow in her adopted country. Living in North Philadelphia, she was surrounded by many other German immigrants. She herself had grown up on a farm with little education except in what it meant to be a farmer's wife and a mother. But with the help of some church people, she got started in a little corner store where she sold everything—fruits, vegetables, and all sorts of groceries. She even had a kerosene tank outside and sold fuel oil.

MERCHANT IN TRAINING

In those days the corner grocery store was small enough that the proprietor knew most of the customers by name. Such was the store that flourished on the ground level of Katharina's little house at 3073 North Reese Street. From the age of four, Charley observed his mother dealing with the farmers who brought their produce to town by horse and wagon. She knew her customers' likes and dislikes and how often they came by, and she planned her purchases from the farmers accordingly, for in those days before electric refrigerators, any foodstuff that was unsold one day, particularly in the summer, might be unsalable two days later.

Payday for working men in the area was Saturday, and on Saturdays the women would come in to pay their bills at the store. If there was a financial problem in a family, Katharina didn't press for payment. In fact, she even made soup for any customers who were sick, dispatching her son Charley to take it to them.

One day when Charley was about seven, the routine of the grocery store business run by Katharina with the assistance of her children was broken. Suddenly her customers, whose buying patterns were so familiar to Katharina that she knew in advance who should and who should not be told of the day's especially good price on broccoli, were hearing news of special sales at a chain store that had opened less than two blocks away. It had happened in other neighborhoods: low prices, special buys

4

with which the corner grocer could not compete—and eventually the corner grocer gave up. Now it was happening in her neighborhood. Ever since the opening of the two chain stores diagonally opposite each other at 5th Street and Indiana Avenue—James Butler on the one corner and Bill Hunter (later to become Acme) on the other—she had expected it, but she could not know which product would go on sale. Eggs, that was it. Eggs were sold at Butler's at a price below cost from the farmers.

In those days customers were loyal. But how far could loyalty go when Katharina's prices had to be above the cost from the farmer in order to cover her expenses? That was her livelihood. All the children knew that. Since there was no way she could match Butler's price, she stopped buying eggs from her supplier. But she had devised a plan. One day a customer walked in and asked for eggs. Katharina had none. But she did not hesitate. "Eggs you shall have," she told the woman. "Charley!" she called upstairs, after directing her customer's attention to other items that Katharina knew were on her shopping list. "One dozen!" she commanded. Charley raced the block and a half to Butler's, bought a dozen eggs at the sale price, and raced back to his mother's store. Katharina charged the woman the same price that Butler's customers were paying for eggs. No profit, nothing toward overhead, in that transaction; but she had retained a satisfied customer.

With such ingenuity Katharina managed to keep that store in operation until Charley was about fifteen, when she sold it. There were several explanations for her success. The big stores required cash, and Katharina never demanded payment. Not only did she extend credit, but she was known for her readiness to provide concrete help to anyone in need. Moreover, the hard work she expected of her children, helping after school and on weekends, she undoubtedly demanded of herself.

The demands of the business took their toll on the children, who had no time for frivolous childhood pleasure. Charles Kurz can not recall doing anything for fun. Everything had to have a purpose. His early life seemed to consist of school, homework, helping in the store, and doing errands for his mother. The store was open seven days a week, including holidays, year round.

Once a year, however, when the German immigrants had their big picnic in Central Park[2] they closed the store and went off to that event.

At nearby Hunting Park other boys played baseball, but Katharina saw the ball games as an opportunity for her son to do something more productive. Baseball games attracted spectators. Spectators would be hot, thirsty, and hungry. What better way to put the occasion to good use, she thought, than to sell them ice cream. Charles was nine years old and had an express wagon. His mother had the ingredients and the know-how to make the ice cream.

The distance from the store on Reese Street to Hunting Park was about 1.3 miles. Charles pulled the express wagon carrying a large round metal can filled with homemade ice cream that his mother had helped him to make. It was his first business venture. Katharina explained to him the importance of adding up the cost of all ingredients, including the rock salt required for freezing and the paper saucers in which the ice cream was to be dispensed. He knew what his mother expected of him, and he expected the same of himself. The total sales must at least equal, and hopefully exceed, the total costs. He could only guess how many "milk balls" could be scooped out of the can and thus how much to charge for each.

It was a hot summer day, and Charles was well aware that ice cream melts quickly. He reached the park as planned, about forty-five minutes after the start of the game, and made his way to the baseball diamond. The crowd of spectators far exceeded the capacity of the small bleachers, and, as usual, many of those who didn't have seats were milling around, paying little attention to the game. Charles selected a likely spot, parked his express wagon, and set up his simple hand-lettered sign: "Ice Cold Milk Balls 3¢." The first few spectators who came by glanced at Charles and the can with its thin layer of frost, and walked on. After what seemed a lifetime, but actually was only a few minutes, one man stopped.

"That's a pretty high price there, young fellow. How big are them milk balls anyway?" he asked.

"Just let me show you!" was the immediate reply. Almost be-

---

[2]Central Park was located on 5th Street below Wyoming Avenue, near a German Catholic church. The park no longer exists.

fore his words were out, he had one ordinary scoop in a saucer. Charles sensed a need to do something special to make this sale. He reached back to the can for a second scoop, nearly as large, to add to the first.

"Now that's some milk ball," said the man. "I'll take it." Charles's heart was pounding. Had he given the man too much for three cents? There wasn't much time to think about it, for in a moment two older boys who had observed the first transaction were in front of Charles each demanding the same size milk ball as the first customer. Word spread. A line formed. Within half an hour Charles was sold out with virtually no loss from melting.

Selling ice cream whenever there was a baseball game turned out to be a profitable enterprise for Charles. Later he expanded his offerings to include the sale of candies and the like, and he continued the operation during the summers until he was twelve years old.

Charles's mother never took a vacation. There was never any excess money to go off and have a good time with. Even Charles's bicycle was used only for a purpose—for transportation or errands for his mother. Over roads of dirt, stone, or brick—in those days few were paved—Charles's bicycle was the vehicle for the family business.

For several years Charles used his bicycle to deliver newspapers from house to house along his street. Before school he had some thirty copies of the morning paper, the *Public Ledger*, to deliver. Only about one-third as many people bought the *Philadelphia Record*, which he delivered in the evening. Each was published daily and cost two cents. The delivery boy earned one cent on each.[3]

The delivery of newspapers was a year-round project; the ice cream sales, strictly seasonal. Although Charles himself refused to use the word "fun" to describe these projects, and they surely contained little of what most young people eight decades later would call fun, they did indeed provide him with a pleasurable

---

[3]The *Public Ledger* in 1898 was a morning paper published six days per week and, according to its masthead, served by carriers to subscribers for 12 cents a week payable to the carriers.

feeling of achievement and the satisfaction that the profit he earned made a small but definite contribution to the family's welfare.

Charles recalls two other jobs that he did while still a schoolboy. One was assisting an undertaker in packing bodies with ice, for which he was paid perhaps a quarter. The other was giving haircuts to boys whose parents were customers of his mother's store. He would go to their homes to do the cutting and, since times were hard and he was only a boy without a barber's training, he did not charge. Katharina, it seems, was far ahead of her time, providing in a small but more personal way through that service what rebates, discount coupons, and gift premiums do today.

A TOUGH CUSTOMER

"That's just like my mother used to make!" Charles Kurz could give no higher praise than to compare some choice dish with the way his mother used to cook. In Germany Katharina had been second cook to the King of Baden, and the quality of her cooking transcended the limited food budget. During hard times, her family's meals consisted of little else than potato soup. Yet there was something about his mother's cooking, especially her soup, that kept fond gustatory memories alive for the rest of his life. In better times there was pork, veal, chicken, or fish and sometimes German spaetzles. Beef, however, was a luxury item that appeared very infrequently on his family's table.

When it came to food purchases, Katharina taught Charles to buy wisely. Often she sent him to the German butcher shop on 5th Street between Indiana Avenue and Cambria Street, two blocks from their home and store. Of the many occasions when he was sent there, Charles recalls two in particular. Both involved pork chops, which in those days cost about seven or eight cents a pound.

Charles arrived at the butcher shop one afternoon after school with instructions to buy two and one-half pounds of pork chops. He spoke German to the butcher, just as he did to his mother at home most of the time. The butcher proceeded to take the meat from the rack, cut, weigh, and wrap the chops in a manner that Charles assumed would be satisfactory to his mother. Katharina, however, was not at all pleased with the goods that Charles brought home. "Do you see all the fat that's on here?" she exclaimed. "I didn't send you to buy fat! If I had wanted fat, I would have told you to get lard. That costs half as much— four cents a pound, instead of eight for pork chops. So you take them right back."

Charles took them back. The butcher trimmed the fat off and gave him two additional pork chops for the same price. Then he brought them home. This time the chops met with Katharina's approval, but she probed her son further. "Now, why couldn't you have thought of that yourself? You know we don't eat fat."

The butcher, who knew Charles's mother and was quite aware that she was particular about her purchases, laughed off that incident. Only a few months later, however, he was chagrined to see the same lad standing in front of his counter not fifteen minutes after having sold him an order of pork chops.

"My mom," Charles began, "she won't take these."

The butcher looked pained. "Not again!"

Charles hesitated. "My mother says she won't eat these."

"What's wrong with them this time?

"She says they stink."

"Okay, give them to me. So, what do you want for them?"

"We want pork chops that don't stink," he replied.

The butcher went to remake the order, wrapped it up in paper, and told Charles, "Here, take that home. And tell her her ass stinks too!"

Katharina took seriously the words of her minister, George A. Sheer, and one of the principles he taught was that the members of his congregation constituted a community and should be supportive to each other. In practical terms, that meant patronizing each other's businesses, and for the most part Katharina did just that. Only when it came to clothing did her path diverge from that taught by Pastor Sheer.

On the first Monday morning after schools had closed for the summer Katharina was up early, saw that the family ate a hearty breakfast, and started out on a journey with Charles. Her store would open as usual with the older children, Mary and Lizzie, in charge until Katharina's return. Before 7:00 A.M. she and Charles boarded the horse-drawn trolley car at 6th and Clearfield (3100 North) for the trip to 5th and South Streets (600 South). The trip took nearly an hour and cost a nickel for each of them. Katharina took the trolley only on those rare occasions when there was an objective important enough to warrant such an expenditure. The objective was a new suit for Charles. Although there were some clothing stores close to home, about three blocks away, their prices were higher than down at South Street. The local merchants had to pay a certain price themselves for suits, and they had to make a profit after that. At South Street, however, the customer who took the time to go there could buy directly from the wholesaler.

The horse car rattled slowly along 6th Street toward downtown Philadelphia. The sides of the car were open, and the passengers sat on benches facing the outside with their backs toward the center of the car, much like the front section of some of the cable cars still in operation in San Francisco. The clattering of hoofs and the wheels of horse-drawn wagons on the cobblestone street made conversation almost impossible, but Charles dreamed of what his new suit would look like and how proud he would be to wear it to church on Sunday. He also tried to imagine what it would be like to have his own baseball bat, for he had heard that with the purchase of a new suit from a clothing store on South Street, boys were often given a bat.

Katharina was convinced that the Jewish clothing merchants on South Street always favored the first customer to arrive on a Monday morning. To get the very best deal, you had to be there when the store was opening. Katharina acted on that belief; when Snellenberg's at 5th and South opened their door at eight o'clock, she and her son were the first to step inside. Katharina informed the salesman of her wishes, and he eagerly brought out several suits for Charles to try on. All had short pants. All had price tags between $8.00 and $10.00. She quickly settled in her mind on the suit she wanted for her son, but she allowed the salesman to put forth his best efforts to extol a variety of suits before giving any indication that she might possibly be interested if the price were right. The salesman acknowledged that there was a little flexibility in his prices. Katharina put forth $3.00 as the most she could afford for a suit in her circumstances.

10

Her English may have been faltering, but her ability to bargain was not. At the moment when the salesman was down to $6.00 and Katharina was up to $3.50, she announced her intention to look elsewhere. She took Charles by the hand and proceeded out of Snellenberg's. Numerous clothing stores were clustered along South Street between 4th and 6th. Although many did primarily a wholesale business, they were usually glad to see the retail customer as well.

They went toward 6th Street, comparing quality and price in one establishment after another. Then they turned back toward 4th Street. The Snellenberg's salesman caught a glimpse of them as they walked past and dashed out to the sidewalk. Immediately bargaining was resumed. Within a few moments, Charles sensed that the suit he had dreamed of was about to become a reality. The salesman went to a stack of baseball bats in a corner and, much like selecting a suit, picked one that would be just right for the lad. He handed it to Charles. "Here, this goes with the suit, you know." he said. "You'll have lots of fun with that."

Charles's eyes widened with delight. But his mother had other ideas. She wasn't finished bargaining yet. "You leave the bat here," she told him in German.

Then she told the salesman in English, "We don't need that bat!" She used the bat as a final negotiating point to squeeze a little further price reduction out of the salesman. The final price was $4.00.

Trips like the one to buy a suit on South Street were rare because of the expense of public transportation. Charles's principal means of transportation before he had his bicycle was by his own feet. There was, however, another way of getting around that boys often used: the "wagon-hopper."

The wagon-hopper was a board with a hole in the center. A rope with a hook on one end went through the hole, and the other end had a knot to support the board. Most boys carried one along, watching for a horse-truck or horse-drawn wagon that was going their way. Once hooked on to the truck, the wagon-hopper became a seat, and the child was pulled along by the wagon or truck. The drivers apparently saw no harm in this practice. Some would even hold the horses to make it easier for a boy to get his wagon-hopper hooked or unhooked from the vehicle.

When Charles was about eight years old, his mother entrusted him with an important errand that required travelling a considerable distance alone. He was to make a purchase at John Wanamaker's. The Center City department store was not entirely completed, but the section that had been built was at 13th and Market Streets. The distance from the Kurz home to Wanamaker's was thirty-one blocks south and eight blocks west, a total of 4-1/8 miles each way, and the wagon hopper helped very little that day. Charles walked most of the way, and he did so in bare feet. When he finally arrived at the store and looked around, he became somewhat confused. It was larger than any store he had ever seen, and he had no idea where to look for the article his mother wished him to buy.

A tall, well-dressed man noticed the barefoot lad looking around for a clue as to where to go. He approached Charles and asked, "Young man, can I be of any help to you? You seem a little bewildered." Relieved, Charles explained what he had come for and was quickly guided to the appropriate counter. The man stepped back while Charles made the purchase for his mother. There was no bargaining. At Wanamaker's the prices were fixed.

As Charles was about to leave, the man who had come to his aid stepped forward and inquired of the salesman, "Are you sure you've given him just what his mother sent him for?"

"I'm pretty sure this is it, Mr. Wanamaker."

"Well, young man, if your mother doesn't like what you selected, don't sass her back, but listen to her. Make a note of what she tells you and just bring this back to the store. Take it right to the same salesman. I'm going to instruct him to exchange it for the right thing if this isn't what your mother wants."

"My boy," he concluded, "I want you to feel that you can come in my store and buy something just as easily as your mother would."

Charles was learning to be independent, precise, and a careful customer. Tasting his own success in sales, his self-confidence grew. The keen business sense of later years was already budding.

Chapter 2

AT THE HEAD OF THE CLASS

While Katharina educated her son through repeated examples of her own ingenuity in dealing with life's challenges, she also valued formal schooling for her children so they would "amount to something." School teachers were to be respected as having authority exceeded only by her own, which in turn was barely less than that of God himself. With this attitude, Katharina started Charles in public school when he was five years old.

Charles attended the Fairhill Primary School at Marshall and Somerset Streets, three blocks south and two-and-a-half blocks west from home. His mother walked there with him the first day in order to complete his registration, but thereafter he went with his sisters or other boys from the neighborhood. The round trip was made twice each day, for the Kurz children came home for a hot meal at lunch time.

Charles took to school like a duck to water. He enjoyed learning new things and worked hard to please his teacher. He did particularly well in arithmetic and drawing. It wasn't long until he established a pattern of being at the head of his class, a pattern that remained with him, in one form or another, throughout his life.

One afternoon when Charles was still in primary school, his mother had various tasks that she was counting on him to do, as she usually did, after school. Charles was always expected to come straight home. On this particular day, however, Charles was an hour and a half late. Katharina was beside herself and demanded an explanation. Charles admitted that his teacher had required him to stay after school for having talked back to her.

"You sassed your teacher!" Katharina exclaimed. "I don't believe it! Don't you know when you're in school, she takes my place raising you?"

13

Charles was an obedient and respectful son who received very few spankings, but he never forgot the one his mother dispensed that afternoon with a stick.

The next morning Katharina walked to school with Charles and found his teacher. "I'm Charley's mother," she began. "I'm sorry, I don't speak good English. I apologize for my boy. He told me he sassed you back yesterday. Thank you, you keep him after school. You forgive us? It won't happen again."

The teacher was taken aback. She said she realized Charles had jobs to do after school and she wouldn't have kept him after school if she had known how it would upset his mother. "Charley is one of my best students," she added. "He nearly always comes out at the head of the class on the tests I give on Friday afternoons." She went on to tell Katharina of the good work Charles was doing in art and showed her some of the drawings he had made at school. "I think he might be an artist some day. Maybe you could encourage him to do some drawings at home." Katharina was reassured.

ARTISTIC TALENT

After completing primary school, Charles attended Thomas Potter Secondary School at 4th and Clearfield Streets,[1] only two blocks from home. There he showed particular talent in woodwork and drawing. Again he was at the head of his class much of the time. To be in that position academically won for the student the right to sit at the desk that was physically at the head of the class. Each week the seating arrangement was subject to change, usually depending on the outcome of tests given on the previous Friday. Academic excellence, however, was no guarantee that a student would remain in the position at the head of the class all week. Unacceptable behavior could send a pupil, amid the snickers of the other forty or forty-five class members, from the head to the foot of the class. This even happened to Charles Kurz on one or two occasions.

The last teacher Charles had at Thomas Potter School was a young woman named Mrs. Hopkins. Toward the end of the winter of 1901, Mrs. Hopkins became convinced that Charles had

---

[1]The Thomas Potter School, named after a Philadelphia industrialist, remained in that location until 1979 when the building was torn down and replaced by a macadam lot.

the potential for a career in art. She obtained for him application forms for a scholarship to the Pennsylvania School of Industrial Art at Broad and Pine Streets and arranged for him to have an interview at the school, to which he was to take some of his drawings. He was excused from school for the morning and made the trip by bicycle, unknown to his mother. Although the distance was only slightly over five miles, the roads were rough, and it took Charles more than an hour each way. Nevertheless, he was enthusiastic and reported to his teacher that they would consider his application.

Three weeks later Charles received word through his teacher that he was among the final group from which the winners would be selected by a contest. The contest was on a Saturday, and Charles told his mother that he would be away most of the day on an important errand for his teacher. Again he travelled on his bike, leaving home at seven o'clock in order to be sure to arrive on time for the contest, which began at 8:30. The candidates, who were all in one room, were given a variety of objects to draw. Knowing there was no way he could attend art school without the scholarship, Charles did his best and said a little prayer that he would be among the winners. Before he left, he was informed that he had won a full scholarship to begin in September 1901.

"Mom," Charles began, "I won a scholarship to study art next year. I can go to the Pennsylvania School of Industrial Art, and it won't cost anything. Isn't that great?"

"How did you do that?" Katharina had a look of surprise on her face, but underneath it all she had suspected what her son was up to.

"My teacher helped me."

"Where is this place?"

"Broad and Pine."

"Broad and Pine! That's impossible! That's too far to walk. And I can't afford to give you ten cents carfare every day. And that would take too much time travelling back and forth. Besides, I need you here. You can't be spending all day down at Broad and Pine just making drawings. Who is going to buy them when you're finished, anyway?"

Katharina clearly had other ideas for Charles. Her last question was crucial; though Charles enjoyed drawing, he didn't have a good answer. The possiblity of a career in art died that day.

15

RELIGIOUS INSTRUCTION

During those years Charles also received religious instruction on Sundays at the St. Mark's Evangelical Reformed Church about five blocks away on 5th Street above Huntingdon Avenue. Such a large portion of the parish was of German origin that the first service on Sunday mornings was conducted in German. This was directly followed by an English service. Sunday School in mid-afternoon utilized both languages, but there was a preference for German.

The sanctuary was on the second floor of the church building. It was an auditorium that seated about 600 people, with a large choir loft in the back.[2] To Charles it was enormous. One of his early tasks in the church required him to be there well before the service to pump the organ. What a privilege he felt this was for an eight year old boy! He was particularly fascinated by the choir and dreamed of some day singing with or perhaps even leading a choir.

He was taken to church regularly, long before he could understand the meaning of the sermons. George Sheer had a deep resonant voice that readily filled the auditorium, a must for preachers before amplification was available. Charles later compared Sheer's approach and personality to that of Robert Schuller or Norman Vincent Peale. The renown that Schuller and Peale attained through radio and television was, of course, not available to Sheer.

It was in the Sunday School rooms and from the pulpit at St. Mark's Church that Charles heard put into words two key principles that he observed at home: that honest hard work would be rewarded with prosperity and God's blessing, and that, wherever possible, one's abilities were to be used for the benefit of those less fortunate. Later in life Charles often quoted the words of Jesus, "You shall know them by their fruits," to which he would add, "and not by their roots." This belief that a person is to be evaluated not by racial or national origins, but only by the good fruit that flows from his life to benefit the lives

---

[2]The choir loft was later moved to the front of the sanctuary, when Charles was about 17 years old, and remained in that location until the last service held by St. Mark's in that building in October, 1957.

of others, originated for Charles Kurz in those early years at St. Mark's.

George Sheer had a special love for children and often took time to visit their Sunday School classes. He knew nearly all the regular attendees by name, and for most he knew where they lived, what their family circumstances were, and how they were doing in school. He could put his hand on a boy's head and congratulate him on an achievement in public school or on successfully memorizing a scripture passage in Sunday School. Each child treated in this way felt special, but the preacher seemed to take a singularly personal interest in Charles Kurz, perhaps because the boy came from a fatherless home. Charles, on his part, perhaps for the same reason, treasured the words of encouragement that he received so often from the pastor he esteemed.

At the age of twelve Charles became a catechumen; that is, he joined the class of other boys and girls of the same age who were studying the catechism and memorizing the answers to its series of questions in preparation for confirmation as a church member. There he sat under the direct instruction of Pastor Sheer himself. As the weeks progressed, each neophyte was expected not only to memorize the material but to give evidence of understanding the meaning of all the questions and answers.

The confirmation took place on Palm Sunday, March 31, 1901.[3] In a special address to the thirty-seven boys whom he had guided in catechism class, Sheer stressed that their childhood was over and that they now had to put on men's shoes. Ida Hartman sang a soprano solo especially for the boys who were being confirmed and its beginning words stuck with Charles: "This world is a source of excitement; there is danger wherever you go." Each verse, after warning of some temptation to leave the straight and narrow path, concluded, "Have courage, my boy, to say no!"

The confirmation was indeed a milestone in the life of Charles Kurz. One week later, moreover, on Easter Sunday, Charles received his First Communion as a full member of St. Mark's

---

[3] Charles was the 2,359th person confirmed by George A. Sheer in the 25 years since he had started his ministry as St. Mark's first pastor.

4.   Charles Kurz on Confirmation Day, March 31, 1901.

Church. Besides being an important day for its religious significance, it was the last day before Charles was to assume a man's responsibility. His mother had been planning for that day for almost a year, having heard the same story about men's shoes from the lips of the pastor spoken to the previous confirmation class. She had contacted one of the division committeemen[4] and made inquires of others as to where Charles could find employment that he could depend on for his future. Her inquires bore fruit. One of the farmers who brought his produce to Katharina's store had a brother who was connected with a Mr. John B. Stetson of the Stetson Hat Company. Employment was obtained there not only for Charles, but also for Matthew Vollmer, a boy who lived across the street and who, although a year older than Charles, was in the same confirmation class.

The family's need for financial support put an early end to Charles Kurz's formal education.

---

[4]A division is a part of a ward for election purposes. Voters of each of the major parties usually elected two committeemen to represent that party in the division.

Chapter 3

"IT'S NO JOB FOR ME"

When Charles Kurz began his first job, it was still more than two months before his thirteenth birthday. Although faced then with new situations that would have unnerved most older youths, Charles was rarely apprehensive about anything, and this new endeavor was no exception. He took the responsibility of being a major breadwinner for a family of five in stride, as something perfectly natural. The need was obvious and he, the oldest boy, was capable of working. Although tall for his age, he still wondered what it would be like working in a factory with grown men.

To work at Stetson's was considered a high honor. The company was known for treating its employees especially well. In addition to giving them Sunday and every holiday off, and even Saturdays after 1:00 P.M., Stetson's increased their pay at regular intervals and gave each one a special Christmas present, such as a turkey or a gold piece. On his first Christmas with the company it was a $2.50 gold piece; as an employee progressed, he might receive a $5.00 or even a $10.00 gold piece. Besides having a retirement and pension plan, Stetson's had a staff that would investigate the needs of employees who were ill and provide such things as food for their families. If an employee was expecting an addition to his family, the staff was authorized to buy certain necessities for the unborn child. Katharina was therefore elated over her success in having her son accepted by such a fine firm and dreamed that he would become an experienced hat maker and perhaps one day an officer of Stetson's.

Katharina sent Charles to buy the biggest lunch box he could find, and on Easter Monday she filled the box to the top, packed some additional goodies in a separate bag, and sent Charles on his way. Dawn was just breaking when Charles, clutching the food that his mother had prepared, set out to Stetson's with his friend Matty Vollmer. They left early to be sure of arriving at the hat factory before the 6:45 A.M. starting time. They walked the 1-3/8 miles to 5th and Berks Streets and found the workers' entrance well before the appointed time.

"What are you doing here, young fellows?" demanded a short bald-headed man who eyed the boys suspiciously.

"We're going to work here," Charles replied. "Here are my papers."

The man chewed on his cigar and looked over the papers. "Looks like you're in the right place," he said. "Follow me."

Charles was shown a small wooden locker without a lock in which to deposit his jacket and lunch. He was then taken through a large room where dozens of men were already at work. Using foot pedals for power, they repeated over and over their particular steps in the process of hat-making. Each of the men in a second room was seated at a table operating a machine that periodically gave off a noisy exhaust of steam.

The cigar-puffing man led Charles to an empty chair and table in a third room. "Here you are, kid. Now let's see what you can do."

The men in this room all received pieces of felt in their natural state, cut them into the shape of the brim of a hat, and smoothed out the hair on the felt. After a brief instruction period, the lad was set to work operating a foot-powered machine known as a brimmer. He watched the men on either side of him, and by 8:30 A.M. he was able to duplicate each step they performed with nearly equal speed and efficiency. The heaviest task, lifting the brimmer, was not easy, but it seemed to present no problem.

Charles strove to do the job well. By nine o'clock he was keeping pace with the workers next to him. The pattern was rhythmic, repetitive, and already growing monotonous. He began to think of the men in the other rooms, many of them older, some ancient, possibly in their forties or even fifties. Had they been doing this all their lives? Would he be doing this all of his life?

At 9:30 a whistle blew. In a moment Charles saw that he was the only one working. The sound of presses from other rooms had stopped. Men were getting up and walking around. Many were already opening lunch boxes and beginning to eat. "Didn't you hear that whistle, young fellow?" one asked. "It's time for a break."

As soon as he got up, Charles became aware of two painful areas. First, his left arm, which had been lifting the brimmer, felt like a dead weight. The other, his stomach, told him that it was time for lunch. He passed a large smoke-filled room where workmen were milling around and chattering, and found his locker. The lunch box and bag of extras were still there. Thank God! He sat on an old wooden bench, alone, and ate everything.

A second whistle blew. His strength renewed and his arm rested, he started back to his work place. Most of the men were resuming their tasks. This time Charles noticed several carbuncles on the back of the neck of one man. The next worker had the same. In fact, it seemed that nearly half the employees he observed in those few moments had carbuncles.

During the next two hours Charles wondered. Was Matty catching on? Did he like this place? What about the carbuncles? Was there a connection between them and the felt?

At noon the whistle blew. Everyone else was soon devouring his lunch. When Charles realized there were five more hours to go and he had nothing more to eat and no money, his ideas took shape. His stomach would never survive until five o'clock. His arm hurt. He didn't want carbuncles. There was no future in this job! He walked out and headed for home.

He reached the house about 12:30, very hungry. His mother gave him a warm reception and gladly prepared him a hearty lunch. But when she realized he had walked out of Stetson's and was not going back, she was appalled. "After all I did to arrange this job for you. And you'd be making $2.50 a week!" she exclaimed. "You're never going to amount to anything!"

"What about Matty? Did he go home, too?" she asked.

"No. He stayed on."

"Now, that's the kind of boy you should take as an example."

In spite of his mother's reprimand, Charles was confident he had made the right choice. "Don't worry, Mom, I've got my bike. I'll find another job by tomorrow. You'll see."

Many years later at a luncheon in the Union League Club attended by many prominent Philadelphia businessmen, Charles Kurz discovered that he was seated next to the president of the

Stetson Hat Company.[1] He recounted the story of his morning of work at the Stetson factory, for which he had never been paid. "That's fascinating. You must have worked for the original Mr. Stetson who founded the company," was the reply. But he did not offer to pay the half day's wages. Matthew Vollmer, who remained at Stetson's and became a foreman, had eventually received a gold watch for nearly 55 years of hat-making.

SEARCHING

The newspaper that Charles borrowed from the next door neighbor that day contained the advertisement of a tailor/dry cleaner who needed a boy with a bicycle. Charles promptly got on his bike and went to see about the position. He landed the job and the next morning began delivering articles of clothing with his bicycle. Within a few hours, however, he was getting that same feeling he had the previous day: "This is no job for me." By the end of the day he was convinced there was no future in delivering suits and told the tailor he didn't like the job. He asked for his pay and received 30 cents.

Charles Kurz's third job was as an office boy at the Daylight Prism Co., 134 S. 4th Street. He was to receive $2.50 per week for cleaning and refilling inkwells, replacing penpoints for the various men who had desks in the office and for the salesmen who were out selling a certain type of glass, and cleaning the cuspidor alongside of each desk. There was no central heat in the office, but there was a pot-bellied stove. Those who had a desk close by were hot; those near the door were always cold. Charles was to carry out the ashes, put in coal, and on cold days make the fire in the pot-bellied stove. In addition, he had to keep the sidewalk clean, and when winter came, shovel snow.

Katharina was delighted when Charles told her about this job. In such an office, she thought, her son could learn how to trade. When he told her about cleaning and polishing the brass cuspidors, she gave him a little lecture on the importance of doing even the most menial job perfectly. If he polished the cuspidors as she thought they should be polished, Katharina believed the

---

[1]Most likely David Harshaw, who was president of the company from 1947 to 1967.

boss would surely notice and remark that they had never before shined that way.

Much to Charles's surprise, within a few days the boss actually said he had never seen the cuspidors polished so well. Charles was pleased as Punch and told his mother that night that she must be a mind reader. She said, "You always make sure every job you are assigned is done well, and the boss will recognize it and promote you."

Nevertheless, Charles soon realized that there was little future in that job and began following the want ads again and answering some of them. After about 30 days with Daylight Prism Co., he received a post card offering him an office boy's job with S. G. Simpson & Co., a custom house broker whose ad he had answered. The pay was exactly the same, but Charles was ready to try something new. He accepted.

Chapter 4

A PLACE TO GROW

S. G. Simpson & Co. had their offices in the Drexel Building on the southeast corner of 5th and Chestnut Streets. Only a half block away, between 4th and 5th on Chestnut Street, was the building that then served as the custom house of Philadelphia, the first of modern adaptations of the Parthenon at Athens.[1] Simpson did the custom house work for various department stores, tobacco importers, steel and ore importers, and the like.

Charles's duties extended beyond those of an office boy. After Mr. Simpson showed his new employee where various documents had to be picked up and delivered at the custom house, errands between the office and custom house several times a day became routine for Charles. In addition, it was Charles's responsibility to make handwritten copies of customs entries and other documents that were required in duplicate or triplicate. Typed documents were not accepted; neither were carbon copies. Forms had to be completed in plain Spencerian handwriting. Charles's handwriting, he was told, had been the best of the some 200 persons who had answered the Simpson ad. Within three days he knew he had found a job he liked.

Simpson himself often took Charles with him on visits to customers as well as to the custom house. Before long he taught the youth how to prepare original customs entries, follow them through the custom house, and obtain necessary permits. The

---

[1]Originally built between 1819 and 1824 as the Second Bank of the United States, this magnificent building with its eight huge columns in front and back, still stands as a historic landmark under the Department of Interior. At present within its walls is a museum housing an extraordinary collection of portraits from Colonial, Revolutionary, and Federal times.

job offered new interest and new exposure daily, and his responsibilities grew.

One of the men who worked in Simpson's office, Harry R. Shultz, also took a special interest in Charles. Shultz, who specialized in arguing against the government when import duties were believed to have been improperly assessed, had taken on the claim by the Cambria Iron & Steel Co. that the government had incorrectly classified a certain new type of imported steel and assessed an excessively high duty. Shultz made an agreement with Cambria and other steel importing companies that if he won their case, he would receive a percentage of the refunds obtained; if he lost, he would be reimbursed for expenses but receive no fee for his services.

The project was an enormous one that required the help of several attorneys and many hours of writing on the part of Charles Kurz. Shultz inspired hard work on the part of all who participated in the case, but he seemed to offer an extra share of encouragement to Charles.

Eventually a bill which resolved the issue in a manner favorable to Shultz's clients was introduced in Congress, passed, and signed by President Theodore Roosevelt. This resulted in large refunds to the steel importers over the next few years. As the checks began to come in, Shultz entrusted Charles, a 14 year-old boy, to take them to the sub-Treasury of the United States, then located in back of the custom house, and have them cashed. On the first such errand the teller asked Charles if he wanted gold or gold certificates. Charles had no idea which one, so he followed the teller's suggestion to take certificates since gold would be quite heavy. He was given the money in $20,000, $10,000, $5,000, and $1,000 denominations and carried it to the Provident Trust Co. at 4th and Chestnut, where he deposited it for Shultz. No one accompanied him. No one thought of a guard. After paying the attorneys and others who worked with him their respective percentages, Shultz netted for himself $136,000.[2]

---

[2]This account led to a confirmation of the remarkable accuracy of Charles Kurz's memory, even in his nineties. The incident had been recorded in 1967 when he dictated part of his personal history to a secretary. I rewrote the story, using the name exactly as it had been typed, Harry R. Schultz. Seeing this name in the manuscript, he struck out the "c" and changed the name to Shultz. When I objected that "Schultz" was the spelling he had used fifteen years ago, he retorted: "I don't care. That was a mistake. I'm positive

A NIGHT SCHOOL FOR POOR BOYS

Charles's own experiences made him eager to learn more about business, and he was delighted when someone told him of a night school that Russell Conwell had opened for poor boys who had to go to work and therefore could not complete their education.

Conwell, who was born of poor parents in the eastern Berkshires of Massachusetts in 1843, had already had two careers, as soldier and lawyer, before he decided to become a minister in 1879. In 1882 he went to a small, struggling congregation in Philadelphia. Two years later, at the close of a Sunday evening service, a young man told Conwell of his own ambition to become a minister, but lamented that he could not pay for an education. He wanted to study, but did not know how to go about it.

"I earn little money, and I see no immediate chance of earning more," the young man said. "I also have to support not only myself but my mother."

"Come to me one evening a week," Dr. Conwell replied, "and I will begin teaching you myself."

The young man agreed. Shortly he returned to ask, "May I bring a friend with me?"

On the appointed evening seven pupils appeared at Conwell's library at Grace Church, and he began teaching them the foundation of Latin. By the third evening there were forty, and within four years, in 1888, Temple College was chartered with a student body of 590 and Dr. Conwell as its first president.

In 1889 the congregation broke ground for a new building on North Broad Street, which became known as the Baptist Temple. Conwell dreamed that some day the buildings of a university would stand on the land immediately adjoining the church. Later the second floor doors actually opened from the Baptist Temple Church, of which Russell Conwell was pastor, into the Temple University.[3]

---

it was Shultz without a 'c'." Which was I to believe?

In the library of the Historical Society of Pennsylvania, I found the answer. Listed in Gopsill's Philadelphia City Directory, 1902, was Harry R. Shultz, broker, 641 Drexel Building. There was no doubt. The name had no "c."

[3]Russell H. Conwell, *Acres of Diamonds* and *His Life and Achievements* by Robert Shackleton (New York: Harper & Row, 1915).

5.   Portrait of Russell H. Conwell, founder of Temple University, circa 1917.
      Reproduced by courtesy of Conwellana-Templana Collection of Temple
      University Libraries.

When Charles Kurz began his evening classes just seventeen years after Conwell taught that first group of seven students, Temple College already had nearly 4,000 students attending regular courses. Catalogues from that era show that it already comprised schools of theology, medicine, business, law, music, oratory and elocution, and pharmacy, the liberal arts college, preparatory schools, a model school, a normal school for kindergartners, physical training, industry, and domestic science for women. The title page of the 1902-1903 catalogue displayed a quotation from Confucius: "Give instruction to those who cannot obtain it for themselves."[4]

The institution called itself "unsectarian" and described its mission thus:

> Courses are given to the young people of our city for a nominal fee, and at hours convenient for those who may be employed day or night. The college gives to all classes the opportunity to rise from the middle or even the most ignorant ranks of society to the highest intellectual plane; and fits them to meet financial, moral and social responsibility as real benefactors of mankind.

The evening department met five days a week from October to June from 7:45 to 9:45 P.M. The fee was $5.00 to take three subjects, one hour per week each, or $10.00 for three two-hour classes. Additional regular studies cost $1.00 each. If a student in financial distress was later in a position to pay, he was expected to reimburse the school for certain expenses.

The 1902–1903 catalogue lists twelve persons on the faculty of the School of Business. They taught such subjects as penmanship, English, bookkeeping, commercial arithmetic, commercial law, telegraphy, ad writing, proofreading, shorthand, and typewriting.

Charles enrolled in the evening department of the business school and attended regularly on Mondays, Wednesdays, and Fridays. He was one of the youngest students in his classes. In fact, nearly all the others were in their early twenties and beyond. Like Charles, they were employed by day, and the majority lacked a high school diploma. Records are available only for the year 1902–1903, in which Charles received the following

---

[4]Catalogue of The Temple College, Broad and Berks Streets. Philadelphia, 1902-1903.

grades: Shorthand 87, Correspondence 90, Spelling 95. His name is listed in the program of the 17th Annual Commencement, June 10, 1903, among 37 students who received Certificates of Study for Correspondence and 58 students for Business Spelling. The expansion of his daytime office responsibilities seems to have prevented him from receiving certificates in such subjects as bookkeeping and typing.

The growth of Temple College in those short years is a tribute to Dr. Conwell's organizational genius and ability to inspire others. Maintaining a special place in his heart for the evening school, he came to visit Charles's class once or twice a week and often made a little speech of encouragement. He told the students that he could visualize them later in life as outstanding businessmen. Conwell's words were a source of inspiration to Charles.

In addition to his duties as president of the college and pastor of the Baptist Temple, Russell Conwell travelled widely to give his famous lecture, "Acres of Diamonds," in which he extolled the wisdom of becoming rich. His biography,[5] written in 1915, states that he may have lectured and preached to 13 million people. From that it was concluded that "probably no other man who ever lived had such a total of hearers."

The students heard bits of Conwell's philosophy, such as "Love is the grandest thing on God's earth, but fortunate is the lover who has plenty of money. Money is power; money has powers. For a man to say, 'I do not want money,' is to say, 'I do not wish to do any good to my fellowmen.'"

In time Russell Conwell got to know Charles and seemed to take a special interest in the development of his daytime work as well as his progress in the classroom. Perhaps this was because of the similarity of Charles's background to that of the first young man who approached Dr. Conwell requesting help in getting an education. Conwell challenged Charles to put into practice at the office each day the business principles he learned in the evening.

THE TYPEWRITER CONTROVERSY

Many evenings, Charles stayed on at school after his classes in order to practice typing. The typewriter had become estab-

---

[5]Conwell and Shackleton, *op. cit.*

lished as an office tool in the early 1890s.[6] Nevertheless, at the turn of the century only a minority of businesses in Philadelphia owned one, and few people knew how to type. There was no typewriter in the S. G. Simpson office, and Charles attempted to induce Mr. Simpson and Mr. Shultz to buy a typewriter. He showed them a letter he had typed at night school, a duplicate of a handwritten letter sent out by the firm the previous day. They were not convinced. Although a typed letter might be useful in exceptional cases, they were concerned that it would lack a personal touch. They were not interested in buying such a machine.

Charles felt sure that, if he could borrow a typewriter from the school and demonstrate its usefulness to his bosses, they would see the wisdom of having one permanently. Dr. Conwell gave his permission. Within a few days news spread all over the Drexel Building that there was a kid on the eighth floor with a typewriter. Lawyers brought him things to type, which he did at night or on Sundays. For Charles it seemed a privilege to stay and do the typing at night and a special honor to go out for dinner with these lawyers, provided it did not conflict with night school. Sometimes a typing job earned him an extra dollar or two, sometimes even five. Simpson and Shultz weakened, but they did not yield.

As Charles grew proficient at typing, he was increasingly struck by the time that was wasted in preparing customs documents in longhand and then meticulously copying them. He asked Mr. Simpson if he could show the Collector of Customs how a typewriter could make copies free of human error, using carbon paper.

"You're wasting your time," was the reply.

"Would you have any objection to my typing this entry?" Charles persisted.

Simpson thought he could easily predict the result, but he gave Charles permission. As expected, one hour after the entry was submitted, it was "thrown out" into the bin for items designated for the Simpson firm. Across the top were two words: "All wrong." Charles took the entry to the head of that de-

---

[6]Christopher Latham Sholes is credited with inventing the first practical typewriter which came on the market in 1874 and was called a Remington, named for the gunsmith firm which took on its manufacture.

partment at the custom house and asked what was wrong with it.

"It's all wrong! Can't you read?" the man chided. "Your boss knows the regulations. We can't accept anything written with one of those machines!"[7]

But when he saw how heartbroken the young man was, he mellowed a bit and led Charles into the inner recesses of the custom house where even an old-timer like Samuel Simpson seldom had been. There the Collector of Customs sat behind his desk and read the entry and the carbon copies. "We can't change the regulations," he told Charles, "but, you know, I do think it's a wonderful idea. Why don't you take it to Washington and demonstrate it for the Division of Customs? They're the only ones who can change the regulations. I think they could be convinced."

Simpson was not impressed. Russell Conwell was. "What do you want to do about it?" his mentor asked.

Without a moment's hesitation, Charles replied, "Go to Washington." But Charles didn't have the money for a trip to Washington, and his bosses would not send him.

Two weeks later Charles Kurz, age 15, was in Washington, thanks to funds advanced by the Reverend Conwell. When he found the Customs Division of the Treasury Department, he was ushered in to someone who seemed to be the chief. He listened to the little speech Charles had rehearsed on the way and reviewed the samples of typed customs forms and their car-

---

[7]*Customs Regulations of 1899 of the United States* (Washington: Government Printing Office, 1900), pp. 124, 127, and 130.

Pertinent customs regulations at the time included:

Article 387: "Entries shall be in duplicate *in writing*, according to prescribed form, and shall be signed by the importer or his duly authorized agent, and shall declare the names of the importing vessel and her master, ... the number and marks of packages, ... the nature of the merchandise contained therein; also the value thereof as set forth in an invoice to be presented with the entry ..."

Article 395: "All invoices ... shall contain a correct description of such merchandise, and shall be made *in triplicate*, or *in quadruplicate* in case of merchandise intended for immediate transportation without appraisement ..."

Article 402: "Invoices must be made out on firm and durable paper *in a legible manner*, on one side of the paper only, and with ink not liable to fade. ..."

(italics mine)

bon copies. Several other men were called in to look over the documents. They were clearly impressed. The chief invited the Philadelphian to lunch with him and told him the idea was splendid. His parting words were, "You'll be hearing within a week and a half that typed entries and carbon copies will be accepted from now on."

One week later all United States Collectors of Customs received a telegram granting that authority.[8]

Dr. Conwell congratulated Charles and exhorted others in his class to follow that example. Charles was very pleased.

The Baptist Temple still stands today on the southeast corner of Broad and Berks Streets, surrounded by the main campus of a major urban university which now has four other campuses in Philadelphia and nearby suburbs and one in Rome, Italy. Temple University continues to hold classes at night to permit attendance by those for whom daytime jobs are essential.

A SUPERIOR EDUCATION

In the fall of 1901 Charles Kurz's mother received a visit from the truant officers regarding his absence from public school.[9] She told them where he was working, and they came to the office of S. G. Simpson & Co. to investigate. Mr. Simpson and Mr. Shultz praised the work Charles was doing and enumerated some of the things he was learning about the business, as well as his Temple evening school subjects. One of the officers subsequently delivered a waiver to his mother, commenting that the combination of his night school studies and office experience was an education superior to what he might get in public school. Katharina was so elated that she finally apologized to her son

---

[8]I have been unsuccessful in determining an exact date for this event.

[9]The Compulsory Education Act of 1895, signed by Governor Hasting, stated, "... every parent, guardian or other person of this Commonwealth, having control or charge of a child or children *between the ages of eight and thirteen years*, shall be required to send such child or children to a school in which the common English branches are taught ..."

John Trevor Custis, *The Public Schools of Philadelphia* (Philadelphia: Burk and McFetridge Co., 1897).

for what she had said when he walked out of the Stetson hat factory.

That incident confirmed for Charles Kurz that he had found the right place for himself. He was determined to learn all he could about the business and the reasons behind the things that were done at the custom house.

Chapter 5

SCOUTING FOR NEW CUSTOMERS

Although S. G. Simpson & Co. had accounts with some excellent customers, Charles sensed that very little effort was made to develop new accounts. Eventually he discovered three ways of identifying potential customers. First, before the arrival of a ship, its owner or his agent posted a manifest at the custom house listing not only the vessel's cargo but the names of importers as well. Second, the names of importers who were expecting goods being sent in bond to Philadelphia from other ports of entry were at times called out from a list by the Deputy Collector of Customs. Third, the New York *Journal of Commerce* listed the manifests of all ships arriving in New York, including names of importers.

Before long Charles could spot a new name in such lists—a potential new account. Few offices had telephones. Yellow pages were unheard of. But there was a business directory from which Charles obtained addresses. He traveled by horsecar or, if possible, by one of the few electric streetcars then in operation, to contact new importers in the Philadelphia area. He met these potential customers wearing the short pants that were typical dress for teenage boys at the time and patches that reflected his family's economic situation. His mother believed, however, that with combed hair and clean clothes he could get anywhere, despite the patches.

In fact, most of the merchants Charles approached welcomed him, seemed sympathetic to his efforts, and were eager to help a young boy get along. Securing his first new customer was a great milestone for Charles. His bosses rewarded him with a raise of 50 cents a week.

Charles became known as a hard-working boy at the custom

house and among other custom house brokers and ship agents. Customs officials, including the collector and deputy collector, were happy to help him. He made a special effort to find more new customers on the premise that enough new customers would warrant his employers hiring additional errand boys. He then might be able to bring in Matty Vollmer and other boys, teach them, and help them improve their status. That day came, and Mr. Simpson gave Charles authority to select another errand boy. Matty was approached, but he and his parents decided that Stetson's was a secure job, and he would not make the change. A cousin, Harry Heck, did accept and caught on quickly to the job's requirements. Charles dreamed of building a business large enough that any boy in the family who was willing to work could find steady employment.

THE NEW YORK GAMBLE

Spurred on by his success in getting new customers in Philadelphia, Charles set his sights on New York. Names of several custom house brokers there were familiar to him. Much could be gained, he felt, by a trip to New York to meet some of these brokers and learn more about importations coming to Philadelphia via New York.

His bosses could not see the point of such an expedition and told Charles that he was too young, that no one would listen to him. He acknowledged that he was only a teenager but gave them a proposal. If going to New York failed to produce business worth double the cost of the trip, they could deduct all the expenses of that trip from his pay. They agreed.

Charles could not wait to tell his mother that night that he was going to New York on business the next day. She told him to wear his Sunday suit, which he did. His sisters and brother were very happy for him. As Katharina walked him to the door the next morning she said, "I am proud of you, and I pray that God will protect you against those bad people in New York."

Charles Kurz was received cordially by all four brokers whose names he had. They gave him much information about imports and exports. At Corsi Zumsteg & Co., for example, he learned about imports from Italy and Germany.

The International Freight Bureau of the National Association of Manufacturers had such a long name that he saved it for last.

That firm had a large office with what appeared to be nearly 100 clerks. The general manager, Daniel H. Burdett, nevertheless took time to explain certain facets of exporting that were new to Charles.

Burdett, who was struck by the boy's confidence and grasp of the custom house business, told Charles, "You are the kind of young man I would like to work with in Philadelphia. I can assure you that you will hear from many of our members in your territory who export to all parts of the world."

Charles was glowing, and it was still early in the day. He made his way to the New York Custom House, stated his business and prevailed on a clerk to give him a list of brokers. Before offices closed at 6:00 P.M., Charles Kurz contacted about sixteen additional custom house brokers.

The trip bore fruit quickly. One of Burdett's member firms, Phillips Pressed Steel Co., contacted Charles to book a large shipment for export to England. The steamship line had Charles M. Taylor Sons in the Bourse Building as its agent. Charles, who was familiar with their staff from his visits there as an errand boy, discussed the shipment with them. They were very courteous and prepared the booking form for Charles to sign. Then a Mr. John Turnbull, who was in charge of east-bound bookings, examined it and found everything in order. But when he came to the signature and realized whose it was, he looked up and said, "I can't accept the signature of a boy on such an important agreement."

Charles reported his plight to Mr. Burdett in New York, who reassured Mr. Turnbull and persuaded him to accept the signature. The way was opened to build more new business.

BUSINESS IN THE MIDWEST

Charles Kurz was convinced that Philadelphia would offer advantages over New York to importers in many locations. Accordingly, he expressed to his employers his desire to contact potential customers in the Midwest.

Charles's bosses thought they had enough customers to keep them busy. In fact, Charles thought they seemed "more willing to drop their work to follow a passing fire truck than to put energies into developing new accounts." At first, they wouldn't hear of his proposed trip, but he continued to press them and developed an impressive list of contacts—importers, custom house brokers, foreign freight forwarders—in various cities and pointed out his successes in New York. Reluctantly they agreed.

So, Charles, who was then sixteen years old, prepared for his first extended business trip. With funds saved from his typing jobs, he bought a new suit. He called on freight agents of the Reading Company and Pennsylvania Railroad whom he knew to learn how one conducts himself on a sleeper. And, finally, he listened to his mother's advice: "Wherever you are on a Sunday, don't forget to go to church. If you can't find a Reformed Church, go to a Lutheran Church. If there's no Lutheran, then Methodist. If no Methodist, then Catholic. If there are none of those, go to a Jewish synagogue, but go to church!"

Charles purchased the cheapest accommodations available on the sleeper from Philadelphia to Buffalo. When the porter took his bag, looked at his ticket, and showed him to an upper berth, it was the first time Charles had ever seen the interior of a sleeping car. He had to ask how to get up there. When the porter brought a ladder, Charles climbed up, closed the curtains, and went through the contortions of undressing in that cramped space. Eventually he succeeded and got under the covers, his bag still up there with him. Finally he managed to get to sleep, only to wake with a start as someone pulled his leg.

"Tickets!" the conductor demanded. Charles started to get dressed all over again, but the conductor advised him that it was all right to open the curtain and hand him the ticket, even though he was in his pajamas. It took him a while to get back to sleep.

At a large factory in Buffalo the receptionist took his card into the president's office, only to return with a message that the president couldn't see him. Charles persisted, asking her to tell him that he had come all the way from Philadelphia especially to see him and that he thought it was wrong for him to refuse. He added that he had an important proposal that could save him considerable money. Charles suggested that she ask the president how he would feel if one of his salesmen came to Philadelphia and the person he was to see refused.

The president emerged and conceded that Charles had made his point. By the end of the interview the president agreed to try shipping via Philadelphia and having S. G. Simpson & Co. handle his company's work.

As the days went on, Charles grew familiar with the routine of traveling. In each city he obtained a street map on which he located the addresses of his contacts and outlined the route he would follow. Whenever possible, he utilized trolleys. With each new encounter his techniques improved. After Buffalo, he visited Niagara Falls, Cleveland, Toledo, Detroit, Chicago, Milwaukee, St. Louis, Cincinnati, and Pittsburgh.

The highlight of the trip occurred at the main office of the Rudolph Wurlitzer Company in Cincinnati. Wurlitzer imported organs and other musical instruments from Germany and Austria via New York. The company officials contended that Philadelphia was a backward port, no match for the attractiveness of New York. Moreover, ships coming to Philadelphia took twice as long as those coming to New York.

Charles argued that freight rates on ships to Philadelphia were cheaper. They already knew that. Then he told them that in Philadelphia organs could be loaded directly into railroad cars on the very same dock where the ship discharges. Since the organs would require handling only twice, compared with five times at New York, chances of damage would be considerably reduced. Furthermore, he told them, after arriving in Philadelphia, an organ could be released from customs in one day and be in a railroad car the second day; in New York fifteen to thirty days might elapse. Charles wasn't sure about the time lost in New York, but he took a chance on his estimate. Wurlitzer asked his traffic manager to check into that, and luckily for Charles, he found records of several imports that had actually sat in New York for thirty days.

Wurlitzer was interested. He conferred with his associates and announced that he would give it a trial. Philadelphia soon became the port of arrival for Wurlitzer organs.

Charles made numerous trips to New York over the years. He could catch the 7:05 A.M. train from the Columbia Avenue Station of the Reading Railroad. The Hudson River was crossed by ferry from Jersey City to the foot of Liberty Street.[1] He would

---

[1] That ferry line continued to operate, connecting Reading and Central Railroad of New Jersey trains with Liberty Street until 1967, although Pennsylvania Railroad trains began entering Manhattan via a tunnel under the Hudson River in 1910.

leave Manhattan at 6:00 P.M. for the return trip.

Before the days of dining cars there was no way to get food on the train. As the conductor collected tickets, however, passengers who wanted dinner paid him 45¢ extra. The conductor then wired ahead from an early stop to the station at Belle Mead, New Jersey, giving the number of meals ordered. At Belle Mead the train made about a twenty-minute stop, engines were changed, and forty or fifty passengers got off and went to a farmer's house for a hearty meal that included everything from soup to nuts. As soon as the passengers finished eating, they hurried back on board, and the train proceeded to Philadelphia. The same option was available for breakfast on the way to New York on the early trains.

THE TOBACCO SCHEME

Charles was not yet nineteen when an idea struck him about imported tobacco. A particularly fine tobacco originated in Sumatra and was brought to Holland for sale at auction. That which was bought by the American Cigar Company came by ship to the port of New York, where United States Customs charged a duty of $2.85 per pound.

Charles thought he had something to offer in the port of Philadelphia and told Mr. Simpson his plan. His employer replied as expected: "You're wasting your time, but go ahead and try."

Charles located the office of the American Cigar Company at 111 Fifth Avenue in New York City. Barred from seeing the president, he set out to explain his proposal to an office clerk. "I understand your company imports large shipments of Sumatra tobacco from Holland," he began. "You must pay a lot of duty. There's nothing I can do to change that. But I think you might be losing time with your tobacco here in New York, and I have an idea that could save you time and money. You could import the tobacco via Philadelphia."

"Ridiculous!" the clerk interrupted. "We could never use any other port."

At that moment the president of the company, J. R. Cobb, emerged from his office, passed by, and was about to leave. When he noticed the youth, he glanced inquiringly at his clerk.

"Here's a guy who's got a big pipe dream," the clerk explained. "Thinks we should bring tobacco to Philadelphia."

42

"I'll sit down and listen to him," the president declared, and he led Charles into his office. "Here's a cigar. Now, sit down and tell me how you think Philadelphia's going to save us time. Don't you realize that the ships from Rotterdam to Philadelphia take thirteen or fourteen days, but the newer ships coming to New York make it in seven days?"

Charles was quite aware of that difference, but he also knew that clearing customs could involve delays of up to ten days. Once unloaded, the cargo had to be hauled from the pier to another location, put on a barge to cross the Hudson to Hoboken, New Jersey, transferred to still another location, and then put in railroad cars for shipment to factories in places such as Altoona, Pittsburgh, and Chicago. It could take a month from the arrival of a ship until the product was on its way inland. "Every day you lose is money lost," he reminded the president of the company. Charles asserted that in Philadelphia the turn around could be accomplished in five days.

"I can't believe that!" the executive snapped.

Charles puffed the cigar. It was his first, and it felt awkward in his fingers. He explained the steps of his plan, knowing that it was feasible only if he could obtain the cooperation of the Philadelphia Collector of Customs.

Although not fully convinced, Cobb did agree to consider the plan, and Charles was exhilarated when he left. He lit up his cigar again on the train and paid the conductor for a meal. But when the train reached Belle Mead he couldn't look at food. It was a long time before he smoked his second cigar.

Philadelphia was a third class port at that time. Ever since completion of the Erie Canal in 1825 New York had been the premier Atlantic port.[2] Nonetheless, Charles believed that persuading a few large importers, such as the American Cigar Company, to use Philadelphia could lead to a reclassification of the port and hence a substantial pay increase for the collector of customs there. With that in mind, Charles approached Chester W. Hill, Collector of Customs for Philadelphia,[3] the next day

---

[2]*Newsweek*, XCIX, No. 26 (June 28, 1982), p. 58.

[3]Chester W. Hill's tenure as Collector of Customs began on August 1, 1907. That of his predecessor, Wesley C. Thomas, ended on June 14, 1907. During the interim perhaps Hill served as Acting Collector of Customs. It is probable, then, that these events took place in 1907.

and told the story of his meeting with the cigar company's chief executive. He requested Hill's guarantee that a customs inspector would be at the vessel to clear a shipment of tobacco within forty-eight hours of the vessel's arrival. Hill agreed.

Three days later Charles received a telephone call from New York. "Are you the boy who talked to me about bringing tobacco to Philadelphia?"

"Yes, sir."

"Are you ready to back that up with discussions with customs officials, banks, and insurance agents?" Charles was ready. The necessary meetings were held, and the contracts were signed.

Within two or three months the first ship bearing Sumatra wrapper tobacco for the American Cigar Company docked in Philadelphia. Chester Hill kept his promise. The tobacco was inspected, labeled, crated, and loaded onto railroad cars within five days. Duty on that one shipment was $600,000.

Some months later Chester Hill was to be the principal speaker at the monthly luncheon meeting of the Philadelphia Traffic Club, and he arranged for Charles Kurz to attend as a guest. Hill made a fine speech, discussing the development of the port of Philadelphia and all that he, Hill, had done to bring about its recent growth. Charles hoped for some recognition on that occasion, but Hill's speech contained no mention of his young guest. Nevertheless, Charles's success in bringing such an important account to his firm spurred him on to further achievements and eventually, the personal recognition he had earned.

CASH COURIER

In the ensuing years the American Cigar Company continued regular importation of large shipments of Sumatra tobacco via Philadelphia. In order to pay import duties, brokerage fees and other expenses, it maintained an account at the Fourth Street National Bank in Philadelphia, to which its New York bank would transmit funds. Its monthly import duty averaged about $285,000. The government would not accept a check, even a cashier's check, but only natural currency or Treasury gold certificates. It was the responsibility of the custom house broker, therefore, specifically Charles Kurz, to carry the money from the bank to the custom house. This he did with no guard and no more thought of possible danger than if he had been carrying a suit to the tailor to be pressed.

Charles watched carefully whenever the teller counted the gold certificates. On one such occasion, when Charles was to receive $200,000, he thought the man was giving him too much, but the teller insisted that it was the correct amount. The gold-colored certificates, each comparable in size to a modern dollar bill, were put in a brown envelope that Charles then carried the one-half block north and one-half block west to the custom house.[4] When he got to the custom house, he counted the certificates again before handing them to the cashier. "I think you're right, my boy," the cashier said. "They got one too many here."

One $20,000 gold certificate too many! Charles asked the cashier what to do. "Stick it in your pocket and don't say anything," he said.

"But I can't do that," Charles said to himself, "because the guy back at the bank has to make a settlement of his own account."

Charles returned to the office and telephoned the bank, but the teller was annoyed and maintained that he had given him the right amount. "Well, if you find yourself $20,000 short when you reconcile your account, I have it," Charles said, and he left it at that.

At about 4:30 P.M. the call came: the $20,000 certificate was missing. When Charles arrived with it in his hand, the teller was euphoric and whisked Charles into the president's office, and they both thanked him profusely. "If you ever want a favor from the Fourth Street National Bank," they urged, "do not hesitate to ask."

Charles Kurz had earned yet another measure of friendship and respect from those with whom he conducted business.

---

[4]Fourth Street National Bank was located at 133 South 4th Street, between Chestnut and Walnut "on the river side."

Chapter 6

THE LURE OF SHIPPING

One of S. G. Simpson's most valued accounts was L. Rubelli, ship agents. Simpson handled all of the custom house work for the Rubelli firm, which was located about three blocks away, on the west side of 3rd Street below Walnut. As far back as 1902, Rubelli was the agent for thirteen sailing vessels in the port of Philadelphia.

Right from the beginning of his employment with Simpson, Charles ran frequent errands to Rubelli's office. Now and then this brought him in contact with the captains of ships for which Rubelli was agent. Bits of conversations about the vessels whetted his appetite to hear more, and he developed an overwhelming desire to go aboard one. It was a Captain Taylor, part owner of a tugboat, who sensed his fascination and extended him an invitation to go aboard his tug and be on the scene for the arrival and docking of a sailing vessel. Charles jumped at the chance and accepted his challenge to be up in time the next morning and meet Captain Taylor at 6 A.M. at the South Street pier on the Delaware River.

Aboard the tug the next morning, Charles ate breakfast with the captain as they moved out into the harbor before sunrise. Shortly after breakfast he caught his first glimpse of a magnificent sailing ship coming up the river. The tug proceeded alongside the ship, and Charles was instructed to climb the rope ladder thrown over her side. He didn't hesitate for a minute. Once on deck, he drank in all the sights and sounds of what then seemed to be such a gigantic vessel. The ship continued up the Delaware River with the aid of the tug, turned toward the Philadelphia side, and, with all sails furled, was maneuvered alongside a dock. The ship was quickly tied up, and Charles went

47

ashore. The hour that he had been aboard seemed like five minutes.

Charles walked up from the river to the Simpson office at 5th and Chestnut in time for his regular day's work. The exhilaration of that first ride on a tugboat and his first experience with a ship stayed with him all day. He had a hunch that they would not be his last.

A SPECIAL DELIVERY

Ludwig Rubelli was agent for certain Italian and Austrian vessels that came to Philadelphia. One such vessel bore a cargo of licorice root from the Black Sea for McAndrews and Forbes Company in Camden, New Jersey. Its captain had been entrusted by a friend with a package to be transmitted to William C. Sproul in Chester, Pennsylvania. Rubelli sent the captain to Simpson's office with the package. The captain explained that he had been charged to be certain that it was delivered personally to Mr. Sproul.

Simpson instructed Charles to take the package to the Chester Express, which ran daily from 3rd and Market Streets to Chester and at that time consisted of horse-drawn trucks. Despite the fact that Harry Heck's father, Charles's own uncle, was running the trucks, under the circumstances Charles was reluctant to consign the package to him.

When the captain departed, Charles turned to his boss. "But this captain had instructions to be sure the package was delivered personally to Mr. Sproul, and he doesn't want other people to know about it," he said. "I don't think we ought to let the express people take it down there."

"Well, how else are you going to get it there?" Simpson challenged.

"I'll take it down myself," Charles volunteered.

"That's too far for you to go," Simpson objected.

Charles persisted, "I'll get up early in the morning and go by train."

"You're not supposed to be a delivery man for Rubelli's sea captains. I'm not going to pay for your time."

"I'm still willing to do it," Charles went on. "I might meet a good customer."

"We don't need any new customers."

48

Somehow Charles overcame even that objection. The next morning he boarded the train for Chester with the package in hand. Knowing nothing about that city, he obtained directions from the ticket agent at the Chester train station to the address on the package. After a half-hour walk along railroad tracks, he reached the Delaware River at the foot of the street on which the Fayette Manufacturing plant was located. But when he finally found the office and asked for Mr. Sproul, he was told: "Oh, you can't see Mr. Sproul—he hardly ever comes here."

"Do you know where he lives?"

"No. But he has an office at the *Chester Times*."

They told Charles how to get there, and he walked back into town. At the *Chester Times* he again asked for Mr. Sproul. "You mean Senator Sproul!" the receptionist snapped.

"I don't know," Charles replied. "Just 'William C. Sproul' is the name I have here."

"What have you got?"

"I've got a package for him."

"Well, let me have it. I'll give it to him."

"No. I won't do that. My instructions were to make sure that I delivered it to nobody else but William C. Sproul."

The receptionist was anything but encouraging. "I don't think he'll see you. He's too busy a man. But sit down, anyway." She disappeared into the publisher's office.

In a few moments a large and nice-looking man emerged and said, "Are you the young man who insists on seeing me personally?"

"If you're William C. Sproul, yes."

"That's me. Come right in."

Sproul was obviously pleased with the care Charles had shown in delivering the package and took time to explain the nature of its contents. "It's called magnesite. You probably have never heard of that, but I'm told it's the best thing for lining furnaces of steel works. We're going to test it. We it it's as good as we suspect, we could be importing 10,000 tons a month. Meanwhile, it is to be kept absolutely secret."

They talked for what seemed to Charles like two hours. "If the firm you work for can handle this, I want to see that you get credit for it," Sproul concluded. Charles's chest went out. He discovered later that in addition to publishing the *Chester Times*, Sproul was indeed a state senator at Harrisburg.

Sproul went on to form the General Refractories Company, which manufactured bricks used in lining furnaces. As its president, Sproul made Charles Kurz one of the first stockholders with a gift of two shares of stock. The company eventually had fifteen plants in Pennsylvania, Kentucky, and Illinois.

Cargoes of magnesite, usually packed in 220-pound bags, like coffee, indeed came to Philadelphia from Trieste and Fiume.[1] Partly as a result of that business, the Austro-Americana Steamship Company was founded. Later, when Charles worked for the Rubelli firm as agent for Austro-Americana, he was involved for many years in handling the ships that brought in magnesite and forwarding the shipments by rail to the General Refractories Company's plants and to its customers.

In addition to being part owner and publisher of the *Chester Times* and organizer of the General Refractories Company,[2] William C. Sproul had numerous other business interests; he was a banker, a shipyard executive, and a traction official as well. After twenty-two consecutive years as a member of the state senate, his political career culminated in his election to a term as Governor of Pennsylvania from 1919 to 1923. His name was mentioned at the 1920 Republican convention as a possible candidate for the presidency of the United States.[3]

Despite such a busy life, Sproul maintained an interest in the young man who delivered that first sample of magnesite. When Sproul was governor, he would sometimes phone Charles from Harrisburg. "Are you busy tomorrow morning?" he would ask. "I'm coming to Philadelphia and don't want anybody to know I'm coming. I'll take a taxi and meet you at Hammell's. They've got the best oysters in Pennsylvania." Francis J. Hammell's oyster house was located at 28 South 5th Street, right in back of the Drexel Building and very convenient for Charles. After lunch the two would set out for Delaware Avenue and walk along the riverfront. Sproul heard reports of Charles's business ventures and gave him words of encouragement.

---

[1]Trieste became part of Italy in 1919. Fiume, then in Austria, is the present-day town of Rijeka, Yugoslavia.

[2]Sproul was Chairman of the Board of General Refractories until his death in March, 1928.

[3]*Who Was Who in America* (Chicago: Marquis—Who's Who, Inc., 1966), p. 1167.

FROM BROKER TO AGENT

During the years 1902 to 1905 contacts with Rubelli increased. Not only was Charles fascinated with the work of the ship agent, but Rubelli needed more help and wanted to have Charles work part time for him. Charles felt a particular responsibility for his younger brother Gus, who at 14 was no longer legally required to attend school. For years Charles had sought to provide him with secure employment. If Charles accepted work with Rubelli, Simpson would need another office boy, and Charles could recommend his own brother for the position.

Gus thus became the second family member whom Charles brought in and personnally trained to work with him.

Gus Kurz, a happy and satisfied fellow and a diligent worker, became licensed as a custom house broker on June 26, 1930,[4] and eventually rose to the position of Director of Purchasing in the Keystone organization. Except for one period in which he left to go into the trucking business, he remained in the employ of the companies started by his brother until his retirement in January 1976 at the age of 84.

Once ensconced at Rubelli's, Charles took to the ship agent's work like a duck to water. In time he worked up to the position of chief clerk. When Ludwig Rubelli died in 1906, the name of the firm was changed to L. Rubelli's Sons, and his two sons, George and Louis, had to carry on the business. They know less about it than Charles Kurz and had to depend on him a great deal for guidance. Then, on September 19, 1907, Louis Rubelli died, leaving the ship agency to be run by Charles Kurz and George Rubelli. In 1910, at the age of twenty-two, Charles became a partner in the firm.

---

[4]Gus Kurz, Charles Kurz, their younger half-brother, Joseph C. Kall, and a business associate, J. Harold Pelly, were all issued licenses on that same day, all with serial numbers in the 140s. Such low numbers suggest that the licensing of custom house brokers had only recently been initiated.

Chapter 7

CHAS. KURZ CO.

Responsibility for running the ship agency of L. Rubelli's Sons fell increasingly to Charles Kurz, since the remaining Rubelli had little enthusiasm for the business. The day came when, according to Charles, he just "didn't show up any more."

For Charles, who had many well-established contacts with exporters, importers, ship owners, custom house brokers, and the like, the time was right for him to strike out on his own. In 1914 he rented office space in the Drexel Building and continued the work that he had learned as a custom house broker, ship agent, and foreign freight forwarder under the name Chas. Kurz Co. During the next few years he had the courage to pursue a series of innovative ideas that helped his new business to take off and stabilize.

FASTER BY LIGHTER

Not long after setting up his own company, Charles had an idea for which he needed capital. He approached the Corn Exchange National Bank (now Mellon Bank) at 2nd and Chestnut Streets with a request for a $15,000 loan.

The teller to whom he spoke said, "Well, have you got a statement?"

"What kind of a statement?" Charles asked.

"A statement of your assets and liabilities. What do you own? What do you owe? And who do you owe money to?" the teller explained.

Charles, who had never heard of such a thing before, said, "I don't have any statement like that, but I can tell you what I own. I own the clothes I've got on. I've got a Sunday suit as well as a workday suit, plus the little bit of money that I have in the business in an account here. And that's all I have."

"How do you expect to borrow $15,000 on that? You'd have to have some security."

"Well," Charles replied, "I don't have anybody to put up security for me."

"I couldn't lend you any money; but, if you talk to the president, maybe he'll be interested in your proposal."

"Certainly, that's what I'd like," Charles said eagerly, "somebody who's got authority." Charles was taken into the office of the president, Charles Calwell, and invited to sit down and explain his idea. Charles told him that a ship coming into the Delaware River and discharging cargo at a pier, such as Pier 80 South, might have shipments destined for factories farther north on the river, perhaps on both the east and west sides. It was Charles's goal to purchase three lighters in order to make this transfer more efficient. He explained that a lighter was like a barge in that it had no power of its own and had to be towed by a tug. But unlike a barge that could go from one seaport to another, a lighter was much smaller and could trade only in the river. Lighters, with their flat bottoms, didn't draw much water and could therefore go places inaccessible to the ship itself. Yet each could carry about 250 tons. Parts of a ship's cargo could be distributed to various places along the river by lighter faster and cheaper than by horse truck.

"That's quite a lot of money," Calwell responded. "You don't have anything we can count on."

"All I have is myself," Charles told him. "You must have confidence in me."

Calwell wanted to know who some of the young man's customers were. When he heard the name of William C. Sproul, he seemed to smile. Calwell declared that he was much impressed and was going to make an exception. If Sproul had confidence in Charles Kurz, then he ought to likewise. "I'm going to lend you this money now, and I'm counting on you to pay it back when it's due!"

Charles affirmed that he would.

In the beginning, the Chas. Kurz Co. charged $15 a day for the use of the first lighter. The idea caught on and it was soon clear that with Charles's attention to the project more than one lighter could be kept busy. The second and third lighters were

54

bought and promptly put in service. The operation was so successful that Charles returned to the bank before the money was due and announced to the same teller that he wanted to pay off the note.

"You want to pay off the note!" the teller exclaimed. "Why?"

"Because I've got the money."

"Where did you get it?"

"Through the very deal that I told Mr. Calwell about."

"Well, that's strange," the teller protested. "We don't like you to.... We like to earn the interest!"

"I'll probably come back for more money, if I have another deal, but I don't need the money now," Charles responded.

The teller insisted that his client tell Mr. Calwell, which was exactly what Charles had hoped for. Calwell accepted the early repayment of the loan with its 6% interest, congratulated Charles and stated, "When you get another idea, don't hesitate to come and see me. I'll take care of you."

A NEW ASSET

In order to obtain that first loan, Calwell had shown Charles how to make up the simple financial statement that he needed to present to the board of the bank, although in those days the bank president had all the say. When Charles appeared requesting capital for another idea, Calwell asked if his statement of assets and liabilities had changed much. His attention instantly focused on one item on Charles's new statement, a second hand automobile. "That isn't worth anything!" Calwell proclaimed.

"Why not?" Charles asked.

"I don't see any reason why you should have an automobile," the banker asserted. "You won't be able to operate it all winter. It will just sit around and rust."

"I'm already using it to great advantage," Charles explained. "If we have a ship down at Girard Point (near the mouth of the Schuylkill River) and I have to go to that ship, I used to have to go down by horse car from 3rd and Dock Street. Once I got to Girard Point, I had to walk a mile and a half to the ship. Then when my work was finished, I walked back to the street and might have had to wait an hour for the horse car to come along. The result was that a whole day could be wasted on that one job.

55

"Now I can get up at 6 o'clock in the morning, be down at Girard Point and on the ship by 7 o'clock, when things are starting. Even if my work takes more than an hour, I'm usually back in my office at 9 o'clock. That's how I save a lot of time, and as a result I've already gotten some new agency business. I'm way ahead of my competitors.

"Furthermore, if I have three ships to tend to, one at Girard Point (on the Schuylkill River), one at Point House (on the Delaware River below Pier 80 South), and one way up at Port Richmond (on the Delaware at Allegheny Avenue), I couldn't possibly get to all three in the same day by the old method. But I can with this automobile."

"I believe it," said Calwell. "But what are you going to use to run it when it freezes?"

"I'll find something," Charles replied. If government officials could ride around in a limousine all year round, why couldn't he? He did trace down what they used—"some kind of kerosene"—and was able to drive his car all winter.

He got the loan. Another new venture was successful and the loan was repaid on time.

EVENING SHIFTS

At the time Charles Kurz began working on his own, very few people worked at night or on Sundays on a ship in port. Charles went to New York to meet some ship owners and asked them, "Does your ship make any money laying in port?"

"Oh, no! But what can you do about that?"

"You don't load or discharge cargo at night?"

"That's right."

"Suppose I could work out a plan for loading and discharging during the night or half the night. I think I could save you a lot of money."

The idea clicked with the ship owners, and soon Charles was setting up evening shifts of longshoremen to work on ships for which he was agent. That, Charles believes, is how his business really took off. When he first started to work for Simpson, nearly everything came on sailing ships. The ships sometimes took two months to cross the Atlantic, and nobody cared how long it took to unload them. But by 1914 steamships had come in strong, and turnaround time took on new importance. If an evening crew could complete the job, which might take up to ten hours, depending on what kind of cargo they had to unload, a significant saving could be realized.

Finding people to work an evening shift was never a problem. There were plenty of men around ready to work: blacks, Lithuanians, Germans, and Italians. Charles took on anybody and never thought about their race or where they came from. The company used to have a horse-drawn truck that went to their particular neighborhoods to pick them up for work.

When the ships docked, Charles himself was often to be seen at the pier. As agent for ship owners, he would personally handle the payroll both for the ship's crew and for the longshoremen. After withdrawing funds from the Philadelphia bank account maintained by a ship owner for such purposes, he would go to the pier where the ship was docked, and pay them cash. To carry $10,000 on such a mission was not unusual.

When his wife Mary got wind of this, she was horrified. How could he carry such large sums in cash without protection! He must have a gun. Charles protested. Carrying cash wasn't new to him, and he didn't see any particular danger. But he was a married man now and on this matter Mary was adamant.

A few days after purchasing his gun, Charles received word that a mechanical problem had developed during the evening shift on a ship docked in Chester. His presence was required to evaluate the situation, report to the ship owners, and arrange for repairs first thing in the morning. Well after midnight he boarded the train for Chester. He was by now thoroughly familiar with the walk by day from the Chester station to the waterfront, but he had never before been there in the middle of the night. A full moon illumined his way as he began down the cobblestone street alongside a set of tracks leading to the wharves. He was highly aware of all that went on around him. A train of three freight cars moved slowly past him, its engine belching soot. A horse-drawn wagon passed in the opposite direction. Aside from the few derelicts loitering on corners, there were no other pedestrians. The moon was partly obscured for a while by a cloud, but Charles could tell that he was nearing the river; garbage dumped in the brackish water, combined with occasional dead fish, provided the waterfront with its unmistakable odor.

It was nearly 2 A.M. As Charles proceeded along the river

toward the pier that was his destination, he was aware of another man coming in the opposite direction. The street was wide at this point, and Charles walked along the right side. The closer he came, the more certain it became that this large, burly black man was walking directly toward him. Charles's steps became more deliberate. His right hand slipped nervously into the pocket with the revolver and gripped the handle. Mary was right. He had bought the gun just in time. He was prepared to deal with any threats this man might make.

The moon was now unclouded. The two approached, their paths ready to collide. Just when Charles was about to draw the gun, the man spoke resoundingly: "Good evening, Mister Charley!" He passed about two feet from Charles and continued on his way.

Before reaching his ship, Charles threw the gun in the Delaware River. He never owned another.

NEW ROUTE TO NEW YORK

Charles's ingenuity and determination continued to propel him toward new challenges. On one such occasion he was the agent for a ship that needed to be repaired in New York. He hired a truck to carry the heavy machinery that was required from Philadelphia to New York, but never considered the risk of taking such a heavy load over those bridges. Harry Heck and his brother, who were Charles's cousins, were in the hauling business, and Charles got them to charter a motor truck that would be big enough to handle the machinery. He insisted that the truck leave Philadelphia one day and be in New York the next.

Trucking of that nature was unknown at the time. The problem was not at the Delaware or the Hudson; although they had no bridges, one could cross the Delaware by ferry from Philadelphia to Camden or from New Hope to Lambertville. This was long before there were tunnels into Manhattan,[1] but the ferries could handle big trucks. The problem was in New Jersey. Most of the roads there were still dirt roads, and the bridges across the rivers and creeks of New Jersey, Charles realized, might not have been constructed to stand so much weight.

---

[1] The first such tunnel under the Hudson, the Holland Tunnel, opened in 1927.

Nevertheless, Charles was determined to do it, and he made the delivery successfully, becoming the first to run a truck from Philadelphia to New York over those bridges. That opened the eyes of the ship repair people in Philadelphia to the possibility of taking on jobs in New York. "Looking back," Charles later reflected, "I was really an on-the-job kid at that time."

Chapter 8

COMMODITIES TO BUY AND SELL

Back when Charles Kurz was still an agent with L. Rubelli's Sons, he made his first foray into the rather shaky business of importing food-stuff. It was the demand for lemons that lured him to give it a try.

At that time, prior to the opening of the Panama Canal, Italy was the principal source of citrus fruits for Philadelphia. There were several reasons why. Few ships ran from Florida to Philadelphia; the trip from California to the East Coast via the Straits of Magellan was prohibitively long; and rail freight from both California and Florida was expensive. Moreover, it took only about twelve days for passenger steamers to bring fruits to Philadelphia from Italy.

A CARLOAD OF LEMONS

Charles began to import Italian lemons around 1912. Lemons and other citrus fruits were marketed at Philadelphia's fruit auction house, where they were listed by name of grower, place of origin, size, and other information common in the trade. A grower's reputation depended on his accurate delineation of his product's quality. Lemons were auctioned by carload lots, generally on the day of arrival of the ship. On the hottest days lemons were in demand for lemonade and brought the best price.

A particular carload of lemons imported by Charles Kurz was due to arrive on May 1. The last three days of April had been unseasonably hot. On the day the ship reached port, however, the temperature dropped about 25°. At the auction house, just before his lot was scheduled for auction, Charles discovered that the price of lemons had already taken a serious plunge of about

61

$1.00 per crate. He conceived a plan of action. In spite of having no time to determine its feasibility, he decided it was worth the risk. He withdrew his shipment of lemons from the market.

Knowing hot weather was predicted for Buffalo, Charles rushed to Reading Terminal and contacted the freight traffic manager, John Hewitt. "I've got a carload of lemons that needs to be on its way to Buffalo by tonight," he stated.

"Too late! Can't be done," was Hewitt's response.

Charles was not in the habit of taking "no" for an answer. "Why not?" he retorted. "There must be some way we could work it out." Then an idea struck him. "How about taking this car up to Wayne Junction and hooking it onto your night train to Buffalo when it comes through?"

"I hadn't thought of that," Hewitt admitted. "It's going to cost you something to get your car up to Wayne Junction, but it might work. I'll get on it right away!" Then he added, "How come you know so much about this business anyway?"

Fortunately, the weather prediction for Buffalo proved accurate. When the lemons arrived, the price there was so much better than in Philadelphia that the difference far exceeded the cost of the rail freight.

Charles gained valuable experience with the importation of lemons, but it was a business with high risks. The vagaries of the market demanded almost constant monitoring. Furthermore, the opening of the Panama Canal in 1914 soon cleared the way for California citrus fruits to be delivered on the East Coast at a price competitive with those from Italy. Charles's lemon importation came to an end.

PEAS AND CUES

Several years later, as head of his own business, Charles decided to venture into food importation again. When word of a green pea shortage reached his ear, he was ready to act. He attended a meeting of wholesale grocers where it seemed that everybody needed peas. The shortage not only touched Philadelphia and New York but spread up and down the Atlantic Coast. He cabled his contacts in Europe and requested price quotations and samples of peas from Hamburg, Paris, Constantinople, Trieste, Athens, and other cities. Having little available cash, he could not afford to gamble and have the shipment get to Philadelphia without somebody to deliver it to, he had to sell goods before they arrived.

Charles's next step, therefore, was to approach the wholesale grocers, most of whom were delighted with the prospect. Some placed orders for five hundred bags, others for five thousand bags. All the buyers reserved the right to cancel their orders if the peas failed to reach the United States by a certain date. There was soon more business than Charles could handle, and some orders had to be turned down. With his orders in hand, there was no problem getting the bank's backing to pay for the peas.

Only one shipment of peas arrived after the deadline—the one from France. The day after the peas were delivered, the Kurz company got word that one grocer refused to accept his entire order and wouldn't pay for it because one of the bags was "full of weevils." Charles, who had never before heard of weevils,[1] apologized and took the shipment back. Quickly his men took the peas and ran around to other grocers and sold a hundred bags here, two hundred bags there, until they got rid of the whole shipment. Although none of the other buyers complained, the incident put a damper on Charles's enthusiasm for food importation.

A CERTAIN NEW CHEMICAL

Just before World War I Charles received a cable from a business contact in Germany stating that they were in the market to buy a large quantity of a certain chemical. Unable to get any offers, they wondered if Kurz knew anyone in the United States from whom they could purchase this particular scarce commodity. Seeing a chance to make some money, Charles called several people he thought might know about it. No one knew anything, but one fellow suggested that Thomas Edison would be the man most likely to know where that chemical was produced. Possibly he was producing it himself.

---

[1]These were a type of beetle larvae which live and feed in seeds, especially those of legumes.

Charles picked up the telephone and called Thomas Edison, expecting to talk to someone in his office. To his surprise, in a moment Thomas Edison himself was on the other end of the line telling him, "Yes, I know all about that, but I can't discuss it on the phone. You'll have to come up here to see me. When can you come?"

"I'll be there tomorrow morning." Charles replied.

The following morning he went by train to Newark and hired a car to take him to the Edison Laboratory in West Orange.[2] The cab driver tried to discourage him. "You're going to have trouble getting in there," he said. "Nobody's permitted in that plant."

Charles told him that he had an appointment with Mr. Edison himself. When they reached the gate, they found that Edison had left word that Charles Kurz was to be admitted and shown directly to his office.

Edison quickly put his visitor at ease and told him he was curious as to how he had become interested in this substance.

When Charles had explained the origin of the request, Edison sat back. "Now that you've told me your story," he said, "I'll tell you my story. Yes, I could manufacture that. We could make a lot of money on it. But I'm so busy producing things that are helpful to humanity that I've made up my mind to have no part whatsoever in producing anything that would kill another human being." Until that moment, Charles had had no idea that the chemical might be used in warfare.

Edison, who was in his late 60s at the time, had great difficulty hearing but no difficulty talking. Charles Kurz was in his 20s, "only a kid really," but the great scientist spent about an hour and a half with him and took him through his plant to see some of his products.

After that meeting Charles did not pursue the matter any further. "I recommend that you have nothing to do with it," Edison had said, and Charles didn't. Like Edison, he subsequently

---

[2]It was said of the West Orange Laboratory into which he moved in 1887 that there Thomas Edison could "build anything from a lady's watch to a locomotive."

A. J. Palmer, *Edison—Inspiration to Youth* (Milan, Ohio: Edison Birthplace Association, Inc., 1962).

sought to limit his trade to commodities that are beneficial to mankind.

It was Thomas Edison who coined the adage, "Genius is one percent inspiration and 99 percent perspiration."[3] He was but one of many with a similar philosophy whose lives touched that of Charles Kurz.

---

[3]*ibid.*

Chapter 9

MARRIAGES AND FAMILIES

During the years when Charles Kurz worked for Simpson, and then Rubelli, he always maintained his regular attendance at St. Mark's Church. Approximately 1200 young people came to Sunday School each week, so many that about half overflowed from the ground floor Sunday School area into the sanctuary on the second floor.[1] The younger children were downstairs, the older youth upstairs. One day, Charles was singing with the upstairs group as the minister walked down the aisle, shaking hands with people. When he came to Charles he stopped and said, "You've got a wonderful voice. I want to do something with you. I want you to get out of that seat and come with me. You're going to take a little class of boys and teach them how to sing."

"I can't do that," Charles told him. "I've never had a singing lesson."

"I'll see to it that you get lessons," he promised. And he did.

Charles not only received singing lessons at the church; he also taught a class of younger boys and became a youth leader. Pastor Sheer knew that a task assigned to Charles Kurz was as good as done.

Charles never forgot one bit of advice he received as a boy from George Sheer, "If you want to stay away from trouble, only go with people who you know will do you good. Stay away from the ones who are up to no good."[2]

---

[1] In 1901 St. Mark's was reported to have the largest Sunday School of its denomination in the city.

St. Mark's United Church of Christ: Centennial Anniversary booklet (Philadelphia, 1976).

[2] George Sheer died in November 1925, after nearly forty-nine years as pastor of St. Mark's. In the following year, about six months after Sheer's successor, Otto Pioch, became pastor, Charles was elected to the congregation's

67

COURTSHIP

St. Mark's Church served not only as a religious meeting place but a center for social contacts as well. Most parishioners lived within walking distance and shared a similar cultural background. Many young people attended worship services both morning and evening as well as Sunday School in the middle of the afternoon. It is not surprising that in this atmosphere friendships grew that lasted a lifetime, even after friends moved away from the neighborhood.

Marriage partners selected from within the congregation were the rule, and Charles never took out anyone except Mary Carolyn Breuninger. Mary's father, Adolph Breuninger, had also emigrated from southern Germany, specifically Stuttgart, and had started a small business selling milk, which he dipped with a ladle from a large can. By 1895 he had a store at 2417 Mascher Street where he and his wife sold milk, cream, butter, and eggs. By that time he had a stable behind the store, two horses and wagons for home delivery, and four employees.

Adolph and his wife, the former Mary Ebner, lived frugally. For every dollar earned, they put aside 50 cents in savings, as Edward Breuninger, used to claim.[3] Moreover, Adolph hired only single men so that his wife could take them in as boarders. Usually four or five employees had their lodging on the third floor of the Breuninger home. They took meals with the Breuninger family and Mary did their laundry. "This brought money back into the family." Once a day Adolph Breuninger took out his Bible, brought along from Germany, and read to the family and boarders.

Later, when the business enlarged and employees outgrew the space in the Breuninger house, it was common practice for Mary to see that a blanket or similar gift arrived for any newborn baby of an employee.

The Breuninger children—Rose, Henry, Mary, and Edward—were each expected to help in the store much as Charles had been expected to help in his mother's store. Among the

---

governing body, the consistory. In spite of the distance from his later residence to the church, he continued to serve in that capacity until the time of Pioch's death in 1944.

[3] As recounted to me by his son Edward Alfred Breuninger.

68

6. Breuninger milk store, 2417 Mascher Street, 1895. Standing in front of white horse: Adolph Breuninger, Mary Ebner Breuninger, youngest child Edward. Standing in front of dark horse (from right): Rose, Mary, Henry.

four Breuninger children grew an intense bond of love and loyalty, and that bond held them close to each other, both geographically and emotionally, for the rest of their lives.

Charles Kurz's fondest memories of his courtship with Mary Breuninger are of their trips to Willow Grove, about 10 miles north of Charles's home on Allegheny Avenue, where there was a large amusement park. To get there by horse-drawn trolley would take over two hours but cost a mere ten cents. One had to stop at various toll gates, just as the people did going by horse and carriage. Only the elite went to Willow Grove by train, and it was a milestone for Charles when he finally could afford the two round-trip tickets from 9th and Columbia Avenue.

"From May to September each year," it was said, "the musical capital of America was Willow Grove Park." Famous bands and orchestras of the day presented concerts free of charge every afternoon and evening. During a one-hour intermission an Electric Fountain display on the lake beside the Music Pavilion delighted the audience.

Constructed before the days of microphones, the band shell at Willow Grove was a quarter-hemisphere shaped acoustic marvel. It served as a giant sounding board that sent music of the big brass bands soaring all over the park.[4]

As Charles Kurz recalls it, Willow Grove was a beautiful place. In addition to the musical attractions such as Victor Herbert and John Philip Sousa and their bands, there were also amusements such as the Mountain Scenic Railway (a roller coaster), the Flying Machine, and the Mirror Maze. Other activities included roller-skating and boat rides on the lake. Charles describes the place as a refined version of Atlantic City. The dress and demeanor of the people who attended the concerts there were very nice,[5] and the food they served at the restaurants was wonderful.

Mary loved the trips to Willow Grove, but there was one person who nearly stole her heart from Charles. That person was Alfred Breuninger, a first cousin who came to visit in August 1912, just after the death of Mary's mother at the age of 52. It

---

[4]Ray Thompson, *Fond Memories of Willow Grove* (Abington, Pennsylvania: Cassidy Printing, Inc., 1977).

[5]Park guards enforced a strict male dress code. Any man or boy found walking about the grounds without jacket and tie was escorted to the nearest exit. A sweltering day in August was no excuse. *ibid.*

seems that Alfred was delegated by his parents in Stuttgart to bring the family's condolences to the Breuningers in America. Both Mary and her older sister Rose were grief stricken. Rose was no longer living at home, having married Richard Souder eight months previously. Alfred sought to console Mary. Her father, unaware of the growing fondness between them, devised a plan to provide proper entertainment for his guest from abroad and at the same time get his sorrowing daughter out of the house to see something new and inspiring—a train trip to Niagara Falls. Cousin Alfred and Mary, still wearing her black mourning clothes, accompanied by younger brother Ed, who was then 18, made the journey at the end of the summer of 1912.

It was soon evident to Ed that Alfred's fondness had progressed to a serious attraction and that he fully intended to have Mary with him on his return to Germany. Ed felt uncomfortably like a chaperon for his own sister.

Charles, who had an uneasy feeling about the trip from the beginning, must have been tipped off by Ed, for he dropped everything, pursued them to Niagara Falls, and won the day. Alfred returned to Stuttgart alone.

Charles and Mary were married by Pastor Sheer in the Breuninger home, then at 7th and York, on Thanksgiving Day, November 28, 1912. Charles proudly took his bride on a honeymoon trip that lasted until nearly Christmas. It was his first real break from work in eleven years. "If I heard of anybody going on vacation, I used to consider him to be a loafer," Charles said later. "But I enjoyed every minute of this trip." Charles still recalls many details.

"We started with a boat trip from New York down to Jacksonville, Florida. Then another boat trip down the St. John's River from Jacksonville through some beautiful lakes to Orlando. As our boat went along, you couldn't see the water because of all the bushes and other vegetation growing there. You just rode through it, like a swamp. Though there was nothing to see at Orlando but farms and orange trees, the trip getting there was wonderful. From Orlando we took the train to New Orleans and stayed at a new hotel. I think it was the St. Charles Hotel. I remember asking for Captain Cosulich and being told to go to the dining room. 'If there's a man eating soup so loud you can hear it in the whole place, that's him.'"

Captain Callisto Cosulich was head of a shipping firm in Tri-

7. Charles Kurz with fiancée Mary Breuninger, 1912. Seated next to Mary is her cousin Alfred Breuninger. Standing behind her is her younger brother Edward. Niagara Falls is in the background.

8. Photograph of Charles Kurz, probably taken on his wedding day, November 28, 1912.

este, for whom Rubelli was agent. Charles had met him some years before when he was still an errand boy for Simpson. Cosulich had wanted some company for dinner and invited Charles to eat with him at the Bellevue Stratford Hotel. It was Charles's first experience having dinner away from home in a fancy restaurant. Eventually Charles Kurz would do business with the Cosulich grandsons in Genoa.[6]

At that point the honeymoon took on a business dimension. After New Orleans it was a train trip to St. Louis and then Chicago before returning home. In each city there were old business connections that Charles wanted to renew, as well as new people to meet.

Mary knew that she was still needed to care for the home of her widowed father and her two brothers. She and Charles thus returned from their honeymoon to live at the Breuninger residence at 2332 N. 7th Street (7th and York streets).[7]

Adolph Breuninger's milk business was expanding. He urged Charles to learn the business and come to work for him. His advice, "You'll always make a living in the milk business," seemed wise at the time. House-to-house deliveries of milk twice a day were customary. A milkman would drive his horse and wagon up the alleys between rows of houses and dip the milk into a container hung from the back steps of his customers. In order to make the early delivery, however, the milkman had to be up at 3 A.M. That might be fine for Hen and Ed Breuninger, but Charles Kurz couldn't picture himself in such a routine. He declined his father-in-law's offer.

Adolph Breuninger's business did grow into one of the leading dairies serving Northeast Philadelphia from their plant at 7th and Indiana Avenue. After his death in 1930, the oldest son, Henry, took over. But Henry was found dead of a heart attack

---

[6]The Cosulich shipping business originated in 1857 with Captain Antonio Cosulich. Callisto Cosulich succeeded in the leadership of the family and later merged his activities with a Vienna firm to form a joint company, Austro-Americana, which started regular passenger and freight services from Trieste to South and North America. After World War II the Cosulich family restored the shipping business and established a new company, Fratelli Cosulich (Cosulich Brothers).

[7]My brother remembers this home as a three-story brick row house with a good-sized back yard. It was a corner house in a "nice middle class neighborhood."

only four years later, at the age of 48. The youngest of the Breuningers, Edward, then became president of the dairy at 40 years of age, in the middle of the Great Depression. Ed paid frequent visits to the home of Charles and Mary in the Oak Lane section of Philadelphia. Beyond his love for his sister, he also needed someone to whom he could turn for guidance in managing a sizable business in that time of turmoil. That person was Charles Kurz. Many were the long evenings that the two sat together on the sun porch pouring over the problems down at "the place," as they fondly referred to the dairy.

A DEVOTED COUPLE

Mary, born on May 2, 1890, was two years younger than Charles, which was thought to be ideal for any couple getting married. But Mary and Charles had much more going for them than proper relative ages—They were totally devoted and loyal to each other. They had an unspoken but sharp division of labor. Charles was the breadwinner and invariably brought home a briefcase full of paperwork from the office to occupy him at his desk in the evenings. Mary was the breadslicer. She provided a warm, loving atmosphere in the home and nothing but the finest, most nutritious meals with lots of Breuninger's milk, cream, butter and eggs (milk having the highest butterfat content at that time was a matter for advertising pride). She took most of the responsibility for raising her three children: Adolph (named for his grandfather), who was born in 1917; Karl, born in 1919, and George, born in 1929.

A notable exception was in the area of model trains, a family hobby that was initiated and inspired by Charles. Early in December 1917, he saw an electric train in the window of Gimbel's Department Store at 9th and Market Streets. It had tracks 2-1/4 inches wide and cars nearly 4 inches high (later referred to as standard gauge), exactly what Adolph needed for Christmas. Never mind that Adolph would be not quite eight months old at Christmas. It was a moment of joy when the train actually ran on the floor of the Breuninger parlor.

Thus began a tradition of electric trains at Christmas, a little bigger and more complex each year. During the week or so

75

before Christmas the parlor was kept locked and off limits to anyone but Charles himself. In the evenings he put aside the cares of business and stayed up late planning, assembling, wiring, testing. In the weeks after Christmas, when friends came by, the men would have "more fun out of the damn trains" than the children for whom they were intended.

That tradition was carried on by Adolph who, when he was a teenager, built trains for his younger brother George. It reached its peak when George was a teenager, and Charles called in a professional carpenter to construct a plywood platform of over 200 square feet in the Kurz basement. George spent nearly every spare minute for six or eight weeks each fall assembling, wiring, and decorating the "Lionel City" of trains and accessories. It didn't matter that houses, people and trains were not all to the same scale. What counted was the feeling of achievement and approval from his father when the task was completed on Christmas eve.

The basement of the Kurz house also contained an oversized pool table, originally purchased for Adolph and Karl and their friends. As George grew older, however, he and his father used to shoot pool together in the early evenings before he settled down to homework.

Charles and Mary always said goodbye and greeted each other with a kiss. When she had a plan with which he might reasonably have disagreed, he would tease her in German, "Wie du sagst, so will ich's haben!" ("Whatever you say, that's what I want!") Underlying their exchange one could sense the deep confidence on the part of each that anything the other wanted was surely going to be for the benefit of the whole family. Never was there an angry word between them or any effort by one to outshine the other.

In 1924 Charles and Mary decided to move their family to a three-story stone house on a hill at 6342 North 6th Street in the residential area called Oak Lane. It was an extended family that included Mary's widowed father (who actually owned the home) and her playboy bachelor brother Henry. Although quite far from Center City and thought of as a suburb, Oak Lane was actually within the Philadelphia city limits, and the Fern Rock railroad station, with its rapid commuter trains, was only an eight-minute walk from the house. Charles and Mary's family flourished there for nearly four decades.

9. Kurz family portrait by entrance to sun porch of home at 6342 North 6th Street, 1929. Standing in back row (from right): Ida Breuninger, Edward Breuninger, Richard Souder, Charles Kurz, Henry Breuninger, Adolph Kurz, Karl Kurz. Seated (from right): Mary Kurz, holding baby George Kurz, Adolph Breuninger, Rose Breuninger Souder. Standing in front of Ida Breuninger: Edward Alfred Breuninger, Jean Breuninger.

KATHARINA'S SECOND MARRIAGE

In contrast to the harmony and devotion of the Breuningers and of Charles and Mary's immediate family, Katharina Kurz's life took on new complications and difficulties as the years passed. Charles's mother closed her store on North Reese Street and moved to a residence at 2230 Fairhill Street when Charles was about fourteen years old. In 1894 she had remarried a man named John Kall.[8] Charles Kurz almost never mentioned Kall. The stories about his days at Thomas Potter School, his experiences at the church, his first job at the hat factory, and his subsequent work experience are all told as if no stepfather existed. The fact is, however, that Katharina and John Kall had three more children. The first, John, died in childbirth or early infancy. Then Christina was born on November 29, 1896, and finally Joseph Christoph on December 26, 1898.

When Katharina's family moved to Fairhill Street in 1902, the three older children, Mary, Lizzie, and Charles, although living at home, were all working. Gus and Christina were in school. Only little Joseph was at home all day. Being a homemaker was not enough to keep Katharina busy, and she was determined to have another store.

Charles recalls that his mother actually operated two more stores. One was on 2nd Street between Dauphin and Cumberland. The other was an up-to-date store at 148 W. Tioga Street, where the new trolley line ended. Electric trolleys came there from Center City, and motormen and conductors would get off and buy coffee or a sandwich from Katharina.

The store was in the front part on the first floor of the family's home. It was a new house with a combination living and dining room and a large kitchen in back. Bedrooms were on the second floor, and there was a fairly good-sized yard in back. But competition from larger stores eventually forced Katharina to sell the store and house on Tioga Street in 1904.

When Charles was 17, they moved to 510 E. Allegheny Avenue, a private home with a porch. Katharina Kall lived there until she became seriously crippled by arthritis in her later years.

---

[8]St. Mark's Church records indicate that Johann (John) Kall, age 30, and Katharina Kurz, age 36, were married by George Sheer on July 8, 1894, at Katharina's home, 3073 No. Reese Street.

When she was no longer able to care for herself, she was taken to live with her daughter Christina and family in the Fox Chase area of Philadelphia. There she spent the final years of her life, at first confined to a wheelchair and eventually bedridden.

Charles customarily visited his mother at least once a week at Tina's home during those years. Meanwhile, Lizzie and her husband Bill moved into 510 E. Allegheny Avenue and helped take care of the house for John Kall. Katharina died on October 8, 1926, at the age of 69. The following year John Kall sold the family home and moved to the Kensington area, where Lizzie and Christina loyally took care of his needs until he died of pneumonia in 1946.

Those who knew John Kall report that he was a heavy-set man who had also emigrated from Germany. He worked in the Philadelphia Brewery at 6th and Clearfield Streets and consumed his share of its products. He was well liked outside the family and readily loaned money to his friends, but he was said to be cruel to the members of his family. One source maintained that he beat the children, though Charles and his siblings deny it.

On a visit to Greenmount Cemetery in 1981 I was shocked to discover that John Kall had lived to the age of 82. When he died in February 1946, I was 16 years old and had never met him. In fact, I don't recall ever before knowing that he had been alive during my lifetime. Having this background, I pressed my father as to why he had never spoken of his stepfather. He reluctantly volunteered the following:

"Well, I felt he was lousy to my mother. She married him, and I wasn't going to leave home on account of that. I just stayed there and did whatever my mother wanted me to do. I did everything he wanted me to do too. Had to do it in order not to get a lickin'. After I got married, he was nice to me."

Nonetheless, when John Kall was out of a job, Charles, then head of his own company, took him on as a laborer, packing groceries and so on. Later when the Kurz company took over Pier 70 North to handle imported salt, Charles made his stepfather the warf manager.

John Kall never deserted the family, but it seems that Katharina's marriage to him was not a happy one. Charles Kurz himself preferred that this book contain no mention of his stepfather. I felt otherwise. Charles likes to give credit to the significant persons in his early life who gave him sound advice and encouragement—George Sheer, Russell Conwell, William Sproul, his mother Katharina. But positive influences were not universal, however, as is evident from the case of John Kall. I am convinced that Charles must have made a decision early in life, most likely subconsciously, not to believe negative things that might be said about him. Whether they were put-downs from his stepfather or anyone else, he would not allow their potentially negative influence to pull him down. Instead, his mind was fertile soil, able to receive the seeds of positive thinking. When Charles heard a Russell Conwell tell his night school students he could picture them in later life being outstanding business men, Charles believed that was really possible. And he proved that it was.

Part II

Chapter 10

NO PASSAGE, NO SALE

From the time that Charles Kurz struck out on his own in 1914, he was eager to charter or even purchase vessels and run his own shipping line.

With the imminent opening of the Panama Canal for navigation, Charles felt that the time was right. He was also excited by the chance to be "among the first to get in on it." Going through the canal would require less than half the travel time for a ship to go from one coast to the other via the Straits of Magellan. Charles envisaged an intercoastal shipping line in which goods could be transported in almost the same time as they could cross the country by rail, but at a far lower cost.

BLOCKED CANAL

From the traffic manager of one of the western railroads, Charles obtained a list of shippers from various ports on the West Coast and began advertising a new shipping line. The Quaker Line, as he called it, would bring the markets of the West and East closer than they had ever been. Two steamships, the *Tampico* and the *Eureka*, were chartered with their crews. Each could carry about 2,000 tons of general cargo. The *Tampico* began loading lumber and other commodities in Portland, then proceeded to San Francisco to pick up additional freight for the East. When she sailed from her third stop, Los Angeles, she was fully loaded and ready to head for the canal.

Meanwhile, in Philadelphia, the *Eureka* was loading with goods destined for the Pacific Coast. Some shipments were from the Philadelphia area itself, but others originated as far inland as Chicago. Even from St. Louis, it was cheaper to bring something by rail to Philadelphia and load it on a ship bound for the West Coast than to send it west by rail. The most notable shipment booked on the *Eureka* was about 200 tons of RCA "talking machines."[1]

The timing was perfect. Both ships would reach the canal at about the same time and be among the pioneering freighters to pass through.[2] It would be an historic moment. Charles dreamed of being on one of the ships and waving to the other as the two passed on Gatun Lake, 85 feet above sea level.

Suddenly word came that the canal was blocked. Something had gone wrong. Charles tried to contact Colonel Goethals, who was in charge of canal construction, but there were no telephone connections. He cabled to try to find out when the canal would open. "Almost any day" was the reply. But the two ships waited at anchor. "Almost any day" turned into "We can't tell when it's going to open."[3] It was a situation over which Charles

---

[1]Edison had just completed a four-year period of work improving the phonograph, which he had originally invented nearly forty years before. His work resulted in the production of an instrument and records that reproduced vocal and instrumental music with improved fidelity and sweetness. Palmer, *op. cit.*

[2]Had it not been for landslides in the Culebra Cut, the canal might have opened in 1913. The first ocean-going ship actually to go through the canal was a cement boat, the *Cristobal*, on August 3, 1914, but this event, as well as the "grand opening" and official declaration 12 days later that the canal was open to the world, was overshadowed by the news of the outbreak of World War I in Europe. David McCullough, *The Path Between the Seas* (New York: Simon and Schuster, 1977), pp. 604 and 609.

[3]On October 14, 1914, a break occurred at East Culebra that completely closed the channel. At some points there were only 9 inches of water where the previous depth had been 45 feet. The canal was closed from October 14 to October 20. Movement of land continued, and the canal was again closed from October 31 to November 4, 1914, and from March 4 to March 10, 1915. *Annual Report of the Governor of the Panama Canal for the Fiscal Year Ended June 30, 1915* (Washington: Government Printing Office, 1915), pp. 27 and 34.

According to one report, the canal was closed intermittently between 1914 and 1916. Significant slides in the Culebra Cut (later renamed Gaillard Cut) blocked traffic on August 7, 1915. Earth masses from either side piled mud and rock debris to a height 65 feet above water level across the canal. It took seven months to clear the waterway. Since this was the only prolonged closure of the canal in its early history that I have been able to document, I conclude that the *Tampico* and *Eureka* incident must have occurred in August 1915, one year after the canal originally opened.

As recently as 1974, the Gaillard Cut was half blocked by a major landslide, but the risk of a major landslide impeding ship traffic is now considered minimal, so long as the present geotechnical engineering program remains effective. Personal communication from George Berman, Chief, Soils and Foundations Section, Engineering Division, Panama Canal Commission, June, 1982.

had no control. He decided, however, to go to the Pacific coast and try to get the shippers together. It took about five days for Charles and Mary to get to San Francisco by passenger train. Once in San Francisco, he was able to meet all of the shippers who had cargo on the *Tampico* and assure them that he had developed this plan in good faith, expecting to make a lot of money. "It's my baby," he admitted, "and still it's yours too, your cargo."

It was agreed that the ship should return to Los Angeles, where the cargo would be unloaded and sent by rail to its various destinations. The shippers knew that Charles had no money to make up the difference in cost; they had to bear the added expense. The loss to Chas. Kurz Co. was in the expenses of chartering the ship. Likewise, they brought the *Eureka* into New Orleans, unloaded her there, and forwarded the cargo west by rail.

A SUSPICIOUS ALIEN

Despite his recent difficulties, Charles Kurz was intrigued by the idea of owning rather than chartering a ship. The SS *John Sharpless* was a dry cargo ship operating on the Great Lakes, one of a fleet of five for which a New York broker was seeking a buyer. As soon as he learned that the *Sharpless* was for sale, Charles set about finding potential shippers who could keep the vessel busy. With a $5,000 deposit, he obtained an option to purchase the *Sharpless* in the spring of 1915 and proceeded to book a cargo of cement to be transported from Montreal down the St. Lawrence River to the Atlantic Ocean and then south to New York. Additional commitments were secured for the *Sharpless* to carry other commodities from New York to Europe. The anticipated earnings from those two trips alone would virtually pay for the ship. With prospects so favorable, Charles took options to buy all five ships from their Canadian owner.

The *Sharpless* was scheduled for delivery on May 10, 1915, in Montreal. Charles Kurz, together with his inspector, a bank representative, and the broker, took the train to Montreal, arriving on the morning of May 8. Headlines blazoned the news of the sinking of the British luxury liner *Lusitania* by a German submarine in the North Atlantic on the previous day. Canada, along with Great Britain, had already been committed for nine months to war with Germany.[4]

In spite of the disturbing news, Charles Kurz and his American companions went about business as usual. They went to a hotel for breakfast. None of them could read the French language newspapers or understand the heated comments between the waiters. Charles visited several different shipping offices trying to obtain additional freight for the *Sharpless* and the other vessels. The other men went sightseeing.

On the day the ship arrived in Montreal they took a taxi to the pier where she was docked. Just as they were about to go on board to begin an inspection of the ship, two Canadian policemen demanded their identification and accosted Charles: "You're under arrest, Mr. Von Kurz. We know you're a German spy!"

The police took Charles to the station house, where he had to sit and wait for a judge. While he was waiting, the seller of the *John Sharpless* arrived and offered his apology. He told Charles, however, that the whole deal was off; under the law, he could not even discuss such a sale with anyone suspected of having German connections.

The hearing that afternoon was inconsequential. The judge listened politely to Charles's story and smiled at the mention of his anticipated profit from the cement shipment to New York. In the end, he dismissed the case and advised Charles to "pack up and get out of the country." "It's too risky," he warned.

"I realize you're just a young fellow with a chance of making some good money, and you don't have any foreign connections," he explained, "but the public won't realize it. Anti-German feeling here is intense, and they'll want to know why someone with a German name like yours is around here buying a ship and loading it with cement. Maybe you're planning to sink the whole thing in the New York harbor and block ships from going in or out! For your own safety, leave here as quickly as you can." Charles did, and he never got back his $5,000.

Back home Charles Kurz was shocked to see his name in the Philadelphia newspapers for having been arrested in Montreal

---

[4]The United States did not declare war until April 6, 1917, nearly two years after the sinking of the *Lusitania*.

as a German spy, suspected of plotting to sink a ship loaded with cement in New York harbor. The headline in the *Public Ledger* on May 13, 1915, read "Philadelphia Man Quizzed as 'Spy': Ship Broker With German Name Taken to 'Headquarters' in Montreal." The officers were described in the article as agents of the Alien Enemy Department of Canada.

The upset to Charles and Mary was enormous. In retrospect, Charles suspected that his arrest might have been set up by the owner of the ship, for no one else knew of his plans to come to Canada. By telling the police that he was a possible spy, the owner was legally able to extricate himself from a sale on which he had changed his mind.

Chapter 11

SALT MERCHANTS

Early in the 1900s Henry Breyer opened a small store at 2958 Kensington Avenue, near Clearfield, where he made candy and ice cream. His business prospered, and he became one of the first to produce ice cream on a large scale. By 1907 he had opened a new ice cream plant at 9th and Cumberland Streets.

Charles Kurz learned that Breyer's requirement for salt to freeze the ice cream was so great that he was buying it in carload lots. Shortly after the armistice that ended World War I in November 1918, he received a letter from a ship owner in Germany stating that he had about 500 tons of rock salt on a ship bound for Philadelphia and that he might need help disposing of it. The shipment was consigned to Alexander Kerr Brothers & Company, a Philadelphia firm involved in the salt business. Charles called Alexander Kerr, who reported that the cargo had already arrived.

"But it's no damn good!" Kerr shouted. "Nobody will buy it. You can take it over, if you want it. Come up and we'll give you the delivery order. But I have to be released. I don't want to have anything to do with it!"

Charles knew what an important commodity salt was. Its use in cooking and on the table was universal, and large amounts were needed to melt snow and ice and to freeze ice cream. He said to himself, "There has to be a market of this shipment from Germany, no matter what's wrong with it."

Immediately he thought of Breyer's and managed to get Mr. Breyer himself on the phone. Charles accepted his invitation to come up and see him and was surprised to learn that he knew all about the shipment from Germany. "I turned it down because it's in pieces that are too large," he explained. He was

89

looking for new sources of supply, he said, because the American producers were "holding me up"—raising the price nearly every time he ordered a carload of salt. He wanted to find a competitor who could deliver his required salt at a stable price.

Breyer gave Kurz the essential specifications and the price he was willing to pay. "I don't care whether it's red or black or white," he went on, "but if you can find the right kind of salt to produce the refrigeration I need, you'll have the business."

Charles found a way to break up the pieces of salt in that first shipment from Germany, and Breyer finally took it off his hands. Then he turned to the problem of finding a new source of salt that would win Breyer's business.

After Breyer told Charles Kurz how much salt his company alone would consume a day, and considering how ice cream was growing in popularity, Charles felt it would be worthwhile to make a trip to Europe. There he could see where the salt came from, meet the producers, and learn everything he could about this commodity. He set about making his plans and embarked in early 1919.

VOYAGE TO EUROPE

To reach his destination in Germany it was necessary for Charles to go via France. The passenger liner *Orduna* took about eight days to reach LeHavre, and the boat ticket included rail transportation from that port through to Paris. Charles would not have been surprised at a cool reception in Germany, so soon after the United States had been at war with that country, but it was France that he remembers as the only country where he was treated discourteously.

"They made me feel like a dog from the moment I set foot on French soil," Charles recalled. The customs inspector went through all his belongings and even took away a little lighter he had brought along. "It's forbidden to carry those things in France," he was told.

"But I don't intend to leave it here."

"That doesn't matter. You buy matches if you have to light a cigarette or cigar in France."

The treatment on the train was not pleasant either. It was about 11:30 P.M. by the time he reached Paris. Charles gathered his baggage, found a taxi, and gave the driver the name of his hotel. Then the driver took him around "the whole damn city" for about an hour and a half until he finally stopped at the hotel. Charles thought the fare was exorbitant, but there was no way he could argue the matter with the driver since he didn't speak French. He counted out the French money to pay him, whereupon the driver demanded a tip. Charles gave him what he thought was a moderate tip, and he turned away to get back into his cab. Charles couldn't understand the words he muttered, but from his tone of voice it was clear to Charles that he was "trying to make me feel like a cheapskate." Then Charles looked out across the expansive thoroughfare in front of the hotel. Something looked familar about the place.

"Where do the trains from LeHavre come in?" he asked the porter.

"Right across the street there," he said, pointing to the station. Charles was dumbfounded.

Determined not to let another Frenchman put something over on him, Charles boarded his train for Hamburg the next day. But when he found his compartment and showed the conductor his ticket, he was told "You can't sit there."

"But this is my compartment," he retorted. "I paid for it."

"Well, if you insist on sitting there, they might let you, but I doubt it."

"Who's they?" he asked.

"The French military officers. They'll come along and say it's their compartment."

Sure enough, the French officers soon arrived and told Charles he had no right to be in that seat, that it was a military seat. "I can't help that, I've got a ticket," Charles replied. "I've paid for this space to go to Hamburg. This train is crowded. I wouldn't know where else to sit, and I'm not going to move!" The officers disappeared. Since they didn't return, Charles assumed they had bullied some other people out of their seats.

When the train was no longer in France, the conductor came up to him and said how happy he was that Charles had persevered. "You know, I'm a German and, of course, I couldn't say anything to them. But I was very pleased you held your ground."

SALT MINES IN GERMANY

In Germany, Charles, who could speak German almost like a native, found that he was treated very courteously.

91

In Hamburg, after arranging some business matters for Governor Sproul and the General Refractories Company, he went to see the salt mines. One of them was right under the city of Hannover. His hosts took him about two or three hundred feet below street level where they rode around in an electric car and saw the beautiful deposits of white salt.[1] Then they took him down to Heilbronn, which was not far from the birthplaces of his parents. After seeing more salt mines there, Charles went to meet his cousins and aunts and uncles from both sides of his family. The welcome he received made him feel like a king.

The trip was completed with business contacts in Holland, Belgium, Switzerland, and Italy. Then, after about twenty days in Europe, Charles boarded a ship in Hamburg, anxious to return home to his family and report on his successes.

PIER 70 NORTH

The business that grew out of the voyage to Europe was so successful that Charles Kurz rented a pier from the City of Philadelphia, Pier 70 North on the Delaware River, to handle the salt imported from Germany. At the shore end of the pier was a two-story brick building that housed an office and warehouse. A sign about eight feet tall affixed to the street side of the building stated the name of "Chas. Kurz & Co., Inc.,"[2] and announced its functions: distributors of Ritekurtz Salt, storage, steamship agents, customs brokers, notaries public, forwarders, distributors, truckmen, weighing, tallying, stevedoring, lighterage.

The pier itself was initially an open pier with nothing to protect the products that were to be unloaded from ships or barges while awaiting distribution to customers. Since salt was the principal product to be handled at Pier 70, shelter from the elements was essential. Accordingly, Charles Kurz secured the city's permission to construct a roof and enclose nearly the entire pier.

A typical salt operation began with a lighter, such as the *Moonlight, Daylight* or *Morninglight*, alongside a big steamer.

---

[1]Two nearby towns, Salzgitter to the southwest and Lüneburg to the north of Hannover, are still known for their salt mines.

[2]Incorporated January 8, 1919.

10. Unloading salt from steamship *Yurimaru* to lighter *Daylight*.

11. Office and warehouse of Chas. Kurz & Co., Inc., pier 70 North.

12. Salt arriving by lighter at pier 70 North.

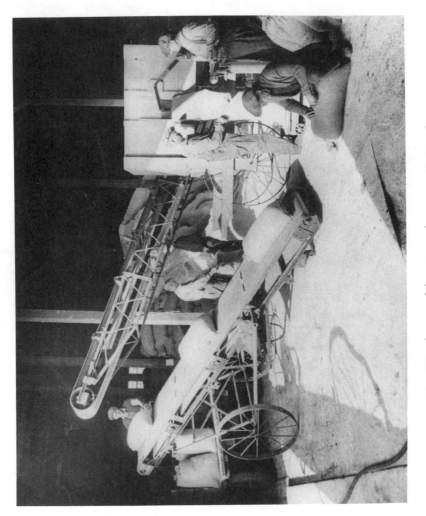

13. Weighing and bagging salt at pier 70 North.

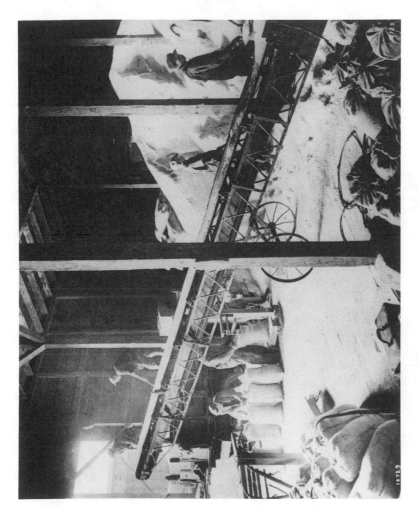

14. View of inside of pier 70 North showing bagged salt, bulk salt and conveyor loading truck with bulk salt.

15. Salt being transferred between trucks and railroad cars near pier 70 North.

A set of cables, pulleys, and winches was used to lower salt scooped from one of the ship's cargo holds with an enormous bucket. The salt was dumped onto the open lighter until it formed piles that were eight or ten feet high.

Once the lighter was towed to Pier 70, its salt was unloaded by shovel (or perhaps with the aid of a crane), carried into the enclosed portion of the pier in large wheelbarrows, and dumped onto a conveyor belt that transported it to the top of a pile twelve or fifteen feet high. The pier had a storage capacity of approximately 10,000 tons.

Distribution of salt began with trucks that drove onto the pier and were loaded by conveyor. Local delivery was completed by the trucks, but for long distance delivery the salt was transferred to railroad cars. Certain types of salt had to be bagged and weighed, which was accomplished largely by hand.

The sign that was affixed to the outer end of the pier and on each of the trucks was more to the point: "Chas. Kurz & Co., Inc., Salt Merchants, Pier 70 North, Philadelphia."

The salt was not only used for the freezing of ice cream. One year Charles also had a contract with the city to supply 50,000 tons of salt principally for melting snow and ice on the streets.

One day, however, the American salt producers woke up and put through a duty on imported salt. Charles Kurz could no longer deliver the salt from Germany to meet the market at the price the Americans were asking. He was in danger of going out of business unless he could find other sources of salt for his customers.

THE BAHAMAN CONNECTION

Rum Cay was a small impoverished island in the Bahamas.[3] One notable asset of the people there was salt, sea salt that was

---

[3]The land first sighted by Columbus's fleet on October 12, 1492, was the island of San Salvador. From there America's discoverer sailed twenty miles southwest to another Bahaman island, which he christened Santa Maria de la Concepción, now known as Rum Cay. Rum Cay is a 30-square mile island with rolling hills and golden beaches. It was among the first four islands reached by Juan Ponce de León in his search for the Fountain of Youth. Its one small settlement, Port Nelson, was home to fewer than 100 inhabitants, as of 1969.

Hans W. Hannon, *The Bahama Islands in Full Color* (Garden City, New York: Doubleday & Company, Inc., 1969).

made as the sun evaporated trapped ocean water. Charles learned that "certain men and a bank down there" made it their business to gather the salt and keep it on a dock until there was enough for a sailing vessel to come along and pick it up. No steamships could get into those areas because the water was too shallow.

Although the uses of sea salt were very limited, Charles arranged to buy one or two cargoes of it and bring them to Philadelphia by sailing ship. The first cargo was sold to various wholesalers the day it arrived. Charles then learned that there was a great need on Rum Cay for lumber and various other items, and he determined to send these things to the island in exchange for sea salt. It was his first experience in bartering.

Shortly after that deal was completed, a committee of about five black men from Rum Cay came to Philadelphia to call on Charles Kurz. They told him that they had been delegated by the British Government to thank him for producing the business for their island. They were particularly interested in the lumber he had supplied and asked if he could send badly needed used clothing and old furniture. Charles applauded the idea. The island people would be helped, and he would have a small but steady supply of salt.

The delegation extended Charles a special invitation to come there, become a citizen of Rum Cay, and live in a home they would provide for him and his family. Charles expressed his appreciation but told them his business in Philadelphia required his full attention. "You could live there just part of the time," they proposed. But Charles did not want to become a British subject, and he knew Mary would never want to live there. He declined the invitation and never went to see the island.

All went well for two or three shipments of lumber, groceries, used clothing, furniture, etc., in exchange for salt. The salt gathered by the island-dwellers, however, was stored in the open near the ocean. All it took was one bad hurricane to wash away the fruits of their labor, and nothing was left with which to pay for the commodities they had just received.

Charles soon decided that this was too risky for him—as "a guy with no capital, to send furniture and whatnot down there to be paid for with salt, and then maybe have the damn salt washed away again!"

A HORSE RACE FOR SALT

Among the domestic salt producers whom Charles Kurz tried to contact was the Myles Salt Company of Louisiana. About two weeks after writing to them, he was approached by a representative of a New York bank that was evidently financing the Myles operation and asked why he wanted to buy their salt. Charles explained the local market that he had developed for imported salt and his present need for cheaper domestic sources. The banker declared his interest in seeing Myles advance and finding new markets for their salt.

"Would you be willing to go to New Orleans to talk it over?" he asked.

"Certainly," Charles replied, "but I don't have the money to spend on a trip like that right now."[4]

"Well, we'll pay your fare down and back."

That was an offer Charles could not resist. He had other business connections in New Orleans that would benefit from personal contact, and he could work them into the same trip.

Arriving at Myles Salt, Charles was ushered into an ornate office and introduced to the company president. "Before we sit down and talk business," he began, "I want you to go around to every department here so that we can get to know you. That way you'll know who you're dealing with too."

"What do I want to do that for?" Charles said to himself. "I'm only here to buy some salt!" He told the president of Myles Salt that he was only prepared to stay one day.

"Oh, we can't do this in one day. I'm tied up for the rest of today, but tomorrow morning you be here at 10 o'clock and you'll meet some of my friends and banking associates."

Charles tried to squeeze in an explanation of his idea for holding down transportation costs by using sailing vessels to bring salt to Philadelphia, but all he heard was, "We'll talk about that later."

The following morning Charles arrived at 10 o'clock to find a group of the president's friends assembled at his office—"big

---

[4]This may well have been literally true, for Charles Kurz's descriptions of his early business ventures suggest that he often operated with little cash in reserve.

shots," he thought. One was introduced as the Governor of Louisiana. All were very much interested in the business, and they asked all sorts of questions about transportation and the market for salt. Charles hoped to settle a deal that morning. Suddenly the president announced, "We're all ready. There are two cars waiting downstairs." Nobody told Charles where they were going, but he went along.

To Charles's surprise, the destination turned out to be a race-track. Charles took his host aside and told him he could not afford to go to a horse race.

"Don't worry. You don't have to pay a thing. This is the best way to get acquainted with people." Inside, he handed Charles $500 cash with instructions on how to go about betting. Charles knew nothing about horses, but wanted to be polite. When the last race was over, he had lost the entire $500 and felt terrible.

"That's all right," the president assured him. Don't worry about it. You'll do better tomorrow."

"Tomorrow! But I've got to get back to Philadelphia!"

"Oh, no! We're going back into the city now, and I'd like you to come to my club with me and meet some other friends. You just plan to stay here until we finish our work."

"But," Charles protested, "I can't see that I'm accomplishing anything! I'd like to make a deal with you."

"We'll get to that. Don't be impatient."

The next day they repeated the same thing with another group of men—the horse races, the $500—and again Charles did not win a thing. Finally, he came right out and told his host, "I'm just wasting time here. I'm going to arrange my own transportation back home."

"You can't," he replied. "We've got all the accommodations tied up. And I've got additional people who would like to meet you."

Charles, who could see another day of horse racing coming up, could not bear wasting time that way. In spite of the president's words, he went to the railroad station himself and found that, due to a cancellation, he was able to reserve space on a train the following day. In the morning he went back to the Myles Salt Company and told the president: "I'm booked on the train to Philadelphia this morning. I'm leaving here without having accomplished a thing. If you decide you want to do business with me, all you have to do is come to Philadelphia, let me know what time you want to see me, and you'll see me within five minutes of that time! We'll sit down and we'll either make a deal or we won't. But there won't be all this fooling around."

"I'm sorry you feel that way about it," was his reply. "You'll hear from me again. There's something about you that we like."

About a month later the New York banker called to announce that the president of the Myles Salt Company was there and was coming to Philadelphia the next day. He wanted to meet Charles at the Bellevue Stratford Hotel at 10 o'clock in the morning. At that meeting, Charles learned that he and some of his friends, in addition to being involved in salt, were the owners of that racetrack. "I'm glad I had that experience and lost your money instead of mine," Charles told him. "But I'll never go to see another horse race in my life."

The president of Myles told him they had been testing him and had decided to give him open credit for several hundred thousand dollars. "Order salt from us for delivery anywhere up to that amount and you can pay us whenever you've got the money." It seemed like a very good deal at the time, but markets fluctuated and soon it was no longer profitable for Charles to bring salt from New Orleans to Philadelphia. And he never did see another horse race.

Charles, meanwhile, wrote to a Pittsburgh mining firm stating that he was in the market to buy "black salt,"[5] a substance that was almost like coal. His letter was referred to a young man by the name of Frank Bolton, who had been delegated by the firm to operate a salt mine in Ithaca, New York. After he got it running, they had difficulty finding buyers for their salt. As soon as Bolton read Kurz's letter, he jumped on the train and came to Philadelphia.

Unlike the New Orleans people, Bolton was a man who could get right to the point. They made a deal, and Bolton's Cayuga Rock Salt Company became the major supplier for Charles Kurz's markets for the remaining years that he was involved in salt trade. Charles sold his salt business to Alexander Kerr Bros. & Co. in May 1929, but the friendship that grew out of that business lasted until Frank Bolton's death in the early 1950s.

---

[5]also known as black halite.

Chapter 12

THE MOLASSES TRADE

Abram I. Kaplan of New York was importing molasses in hogsheads[1] from Cuba and other sources in the West Indies. Among his customers was the David Berg Distilling Company in Philadelphia. In 1912 Charles Kurz was delegated by Kaplan's New York custom house broker to handle a particular shipment to Berg. This meant making entry at the custom house, paying the duty, and giving a delivery order to the buyer.

The importer's invoice for the delivered price of the molasses had to be paid by Berg, and Charles Kurz was specifically instructed not to turn over the documents necessary for release of the shipment to Berg until he had a certified check for the amount of the invoice. "It was not so much a lack of trust," Charles explained, "but that fellow in New York probably operated on a shoestring. He had to borrow the money to pay the shipper. And so he couldn't risk accepting an ordinary check. He had to be absolutely sure of getting his money as soon as he turned over the documents for the cargo." Charles understood this from his own experience.

Philip Publicker, president of David Berg Distilling, had a brother Harry who was in the same business under the name of Publicker-Ward Distilling Company. Both Publickers, it was known, went around from saloon to saloon and bought empty barrels. In those days whiskey was in barrels. However, after the saloon keepers bottled their stuff, they were not permitted to use the barrels over again for whiskey. The Publickers would

---

[1]These were extra large casks containing 63 gallons (twice the capacity of a barrel) to 140 gallons.

take the empty barrels to their little plant, steam out the insides and collect the residual alcohol, which they sold.

Alcohol could be made out of potatoes or other raw products, but most cheaply from molasses. Through handling that initial molasses shipment, Charles Kurz met Philip Publicker and learned of the growing demand for alcohol. Publicker hoped to import molasses directly, without an intermediary, and he was anxious to find every possible source of supply. If Charles Kurz served him well, his firm would be designated to handle details for Berg's molasses importation, which Publicker predicted would run into large quantities.

The two brothers competed with each other in selling their products, but when it came to buying raw materials, both were anxious not to compete. For a long time they were unable to find suppliers who would sell to them directly and had to continue their buying through New York importers. Their dissatisfaction intensified. After numerous meetings with the Publicker brothers and their associates and much research, Charles was instrumental not only in solving the supply problem, but also in finding ocean transportation for molasses.

A CONTINUING RELATIONSHIP

After Berg Distilling merged with another company and terminated the use of molasses, Charles continued to work closely with Harry Publicker and later with his son-in-law, S. S. Neuman. Charles arranged to charter various ships and barges to carry fluid molasses in bulk in their tanks for Publicker-Ward.

The Publicker business prospered. They were making money galore. So Charles talked them into buying an old battleship called the *Detroit* and converting it into a tank barge. They bought a tugboat that towed that barge down to the West Indies empty and brought it back full of molasses.

As the alcohol business increased, Charles became certain that they could keep a small tank steamer busy constantly. In 1919 Charles Kurz convinced the Publickers to have their own ship built on the Great Lakes. That ship, named the *Philip Publicker*, was acquired on April 19, 1920, and, although small, it was as large as a ship could be to go through the Welland Canal from Lake Erie to Lake Ontario. The *Philip Publicker* was owned by the Publickers but operated by Chas. Kurz & Co., Inc. On her first voyage, the ship went to Cienfuegos, Cuba, for a cargo of molasses supplied by the same Mr. Kaplan who was responsible for Charles Kurz's initial contact with Philip Publicker.

Publicker-Ward had to build additional tanks at their docks to accommodate the molasses that this ship brought from Cuban ports and from Puerto Rico. But within a few years Charles felt that the company could use a larger tanker and possibly cut transportation costs in half. About that time the United States Shipping Board was anxious to dispose of World War I tankers, and Charles informed Publickers that he could buy a large tanker from the government by putting up perhaps 10 percent in cash and paying the balance over a period of perhaps ten years. "That sounds like a good place for us to put our money," was their response.

So Philip Publicker and Charles Kurz went to Washington to negotiate the purchase of the *Antietam*. Although not even 7,000 tons, she was considered a large ship at the time.[2] On May 9, 1923, the *Antietam* was acquired and put in a one-boat company: the Antietam Steamship Corporation. Chas. Kurz & Co., Inc., supervised the preparation of the *Antietam* for use and managed the ship's operation. The *Philip Publicker* was sold at a loss.

The *Antietam* was so efficient that it moved the molasses even faster than it could be used. So it fell to Charles Kurz to find other business that would keep the ship occupied. He chartered the *Antietam* to a Japanese firm, the Asano Busan Company, to carry a cargo of oil from California to a port in Northern Japan. Captain Palmgren, master of the ship, took his wife along on that pioneering voyage. Their arrival in Japan, he later reported, created such a stir in the town that local schools closed

---

[2]The *Antietam*, built in November 1919, had a gross tonnage of 6792; net, 4293. Gross tonnage is the total capacity of a ship's hull below the upper deck in cubic feet, divided by 100.

Net tonnage is the cargo-carrying capacity (total capacity less space inside the hull for crew's quarters, fuel, supplies, machinery, etc.) in cubic feet, divided by 100.

Deadweight tonnage is the number of tons of cargo a ship can carry to trim her hull down to her allotted Plimsoll line (a mark indicating the draught levels to which a ship may be loaded), based on cubic capacity, divided by 100. *The Oxford Companion to Ships and the Sea*, ed. Peter Kemp (London: Oxford University Press, 1976).

in order to give the children a chance to see a white man and his wife. The *Antietam* returned from the Far East under charter to the British Molasses Company with a cargo of molasses bound for Philadelphia from the Dutch East Indies. She then resumed the Cuba-to-Philadelphia molasses trade.[3]

During the early years of Charles Kurz's involvement with molasses importation, he learned that in the Dutch East Indies a certain type of molasses was put into baskets, allowed to harden, and then sold for cattle feed. Just when alcohol producers in Philadelphia and New york were grumbling about the Cubans trying to raise their prices, Charles recommended to Publickers and to another firm in New York that they try the hard molasses from the Dutch East Indies. Soon he had orders for about eighteen tons of hard molasses, and he arranged to import a small cargo to see how it would work. On arrival it was remelted, and the two firms were delighted by its suitability for making alcohol.

A minor dispute over what the duty rate should be was quickly resolved, and the way was then clear to charter a ship that could carry about 10,000 tons. The alcohol people were overjoyed by the prospects of continuing to bring this hard molasses from the Far East. They got their heads together and said, "We'll show these Cubans."

But their plans were undermined by the British, who had control over sugar and various other beets in many parts of the world. When a merchant named Kielberg, who owned the United Molasses Company in London, heard about Publickers' purchase, he bought up the entire output of the producers in the Far East. After his one shipload, Charles Kurz was unable to find a way to continue importing the hard molasses from the Dutch East Indies.

ARBITRATION IN LONDON

One of the ships that Charles Kurz engaged for the molasses trade in the 1920s was a French tanker still under construction.

---

[3]A by-product of that Far East trip was Mrs. Palmgren's discovery of an array of beautiful Japanese art objects at irresistible prices. Not only did she bring a collection for herself, but she became the self-appointed agent to do likewise for the boss's wife. That was most likely the start of Mary Kurz's fascination with figurines.

On behalf of Publickers he borrowed a considerable sum of money as a deposit on her charter. But when she was completed and the owners tendered her to Chas. Kurz & Co., Inc., for operation, a dispute arose. The ship was lacking various items that had been represented to be on board. Kurz refused to accept the ship unless the deficiencies were corrected. The owners submitted the matter to arbitration in London, and not until five or six months later was the case listed to be heard.

At that time Charles Kurz "didn't even know what arbitration meant." He had to look up the word. But he studied the case in detail and planned to go to London and handle the arguments himself. Once in London, however, he was promptly informed that he would not be permitted to handle the case himself but needed to be represented by a barrister. Charles hardly knew what a barrister was, let alone how to find one. Then the name of a London firm for whom he had acted as shipping agent came to mind. He found their office and explained his plight.

"That's right," he was told. "You can't go there yourself. You'll need a barrister." They contacted their law firm and arranged for Charles to see a lawyer who was both familiar with maritime matters and privileged to plead in the particular court where Charles needed him.

The meeting was the next day. The barrister was impressed by Charles's command of this case, but reiterated that he was not permitted to handle it himself. "But you'll sit alongside of me," the barrister instructed him. "I'll lead you with questions, and you just state your answers."

The hearing took place in a paneled courtroom with the utmost formality. As Charles Kurz's case was presented, he had the distinct impression that the judge, in spite of his dignified appearance, was bored. Charles delineated the items in dispute, but the judge seemed not to be listening. Charles continued. The judge's eyelids lowered. So did Charles's hopes of winning his case. After all the preparation, crossing the Atlantic, finding a barrister, here he was reciting the details to a judge who was too sleepy to pay attention. Charles spoke louder, but the judge's head continued to nod.

When both sides had completed their testimony, the judge suddenly came alive. He delivered a lucid summary of the merits of the case and, to Charles's astonishment, commended his clear presentation and rendered a verdict favorable to his side.

Charles cabled the report of his success to the Publickers and set sail for America with a great sense of accomplishment. But the story was not over. When the time came to get their deposit back, they found the owners had gone into bankruptcy and lost everything including the ship. The deposit was never recovered.

A FLEET OF TANKERS

To meet Publickers' continuing needs for additional transportation, Charles Kurz chartered ships for them, for which he received a brokerage fee from the ship owners.

Early in 1929 the United States Shipping Board, anxious to dispose of tankers that they still held in lay-up since World War I, advertised the sale of five such vessels. On Charles's recommendation, Publickers gave him authority to submit bids on their behalf; but the bids were too low. When a second group of ships was to be sold in the spring of 1929, Charles again advised a Publicker bid. This time Neuman added one million dollars to the amount Charles had suggested, and they were soon the owners of five tankers. Following the advice of an admiralty law firm, Charles formed a separate company to own each of these ships and organized the Pennsylvania Shipping Company[4] to operate those five ships and any others that Publickers might purchase.

Charles Kurz was paid a fee for acquiring the ships and organizing the companies and a salary as president of Pennsylvania Shipping Company, but he held none of the stock in those companies. He lost no time in finding business for the tankers.

The work with Publickers and their shipping interests, which had expanded far beyond the transportation of molasses for their own use, now occupied a major portion of Charles Kurz's time. In addition, one small tanker that he held on his own, the *Dannedaike*,[5] presented a problem. She was in fact his first tanker, owned indirectly by Chas. Kurz & Co., Inc., through a subsidiary called the Dannedaike Shipping Company, and chartered to carry oil for the Atlantic Refining Company and other companies. Realizing that the *Dannedaike* might be perceived as competing with the Publicker ships, Charles offered to sell her

---

[4] Incorporated on April 30, 1929.

[5] Built in December 1919, the *Dannedaike* had a gross tonnage of 4310; net 2520.

to Publickers. They accepted, and she became part of the fleet operated by the Pennsylvania Shipping Company.

From his Hamburg agent, Charles then learned of a new ship named the *Winnetou*, owned by F. & W. Joch. The ship was available for charter with her German captain, Fritz Steinkraus, and crew. Calculating that the *Winnetou* would provide cheap transportation, Charles closed the deal for Publickers and the *Winnetou* began a regular molasses trade between Cuba and Philadelphia in January 1932. At 8,000 tons, the *Winnetou* would look like scarcely more than a lifeboat beside today's supertankers.[6]

That trade continued up until the start of World War II, and over the years Captain Steinkraus became a legend in the Kurz home. He was an enormous man, with solid muscles and deep lines in the dark skin of his face. It was said that he had to make a conscious effort to restrain his muscle power in a handshake to avoid crushing bones in the other person's hand. For breakfast he easily consumed six fried eggs along with toast, potatoes, juice, fruit and coffee. One summer in the late 1930s, Steinkraus visited the Kurz summer home in Margate, New Jersey. Walking on the boardwalk with his boss one evening after a violent storm, Steinkraus was exhilarated by the crashing of the gigantic waves against the pilings and the spray of the sea upon the boardwalk. Such was the hearty spirit of the man.

Charles Kurz was shorter than Steinkraus and appeared to have the muscles of a jelly fish by comparison. But Kurz was his boss, and Steinkraus rendered unfailing respect to him and to his wife.

The *Winnetou* reportedly was sunk off the coast of Spain during World War II, but Steinkraus survived. After the war he became captain of the private yacht of shipping magnate Daniel K. Ludwig.

STORAGE AT CRANEY ISLAND

Craney Island, near Norfolk, Virginia, was the site of a Navy fuel oil station, slated for demolition. The tanks that had stored

---

[6]Winnetou was a name well known to European children. Their story books contained tales about Indians in the American West by Karl May, a German author, who, in fact, had never been to the United States. One of the Indians he created was Winnetou.

111

fuel oil for ships during World War I were regarded as of no further use. In March 1932 Charles Kurz learned from a friend in Washington about the Navy's plans to dismantle the entire tank station and sell the steel for scrap. They were anxious to get rid of an expense, but it struck Charles that he could use that place for storing molasses and other commodities. This would enable him to take advantage of times when the molasses market was low by buying up large quantities that they previously would have been unable to handle. If fuel oil could be bought for 25 cents a barrel, it also could be stored and later sold for 35 cents a barrel. Moreover, keeping the plant intact and ready for use would be a great asset to the government in case of another emergency.

An arrangement to rent the property at $500 per year was reached the following year. The Virginia Tank Storage Co., of which Kurz was president, was formed and took over the station from the United States Shipping Board under a five-year lease. Some parts of the station had already been torn down; tanks and pipelines were in need of repair; and extensive dredging was required to enable ocean-going tankers to berth there. Dredging brought objections from the oyster people who had beds there, but the Shipping Board helped to overcome that obstacle.

Kurz sent Herman Redhorst from Philadelphia to manage Craney Island. Eventually, at far more expense than anticipated, the entire plant was put in good operating order. There were about ten large tanks for storing molasses and fuel oil. But the economy was depressed and it took a long time to develop sufficient storage business just to break even.

Then, just when it seemed that he had turned it into a successful operation, the Navy announced its need for Craney Island. When the lease expired in 1938, Kurz redelivered to the Shipping Board a fully operational station. The plant had been preserved for service in World War II. Today the Craney Island U. S. Navy Fuel Depot remains a major government storage terminal on the East Coast.

Each opportunity to purchase additional tankers was placed before Publickers. Although some were accepted, the time came when Publickers felt that they had enough eggs in their own basket and agreed to Charles Kurz buying the ships on his own account. The ships would be owned by Chas. Kurz & Co., Inc., but operated by the Pennsylvania Shipping Company along with the Publicker fleet.

Both fleets grew. By 1939, at the onset of World War II, the combined fleet numbered eighteen vessels.

Chapter 13

NATIONAL DEFENSE TANKERS

In the late 1930s both the U. S. Maritime Commission and the Navy sought to encourage construction of high-speed tankers that could be used in the event of national emergency. At the same time, one of Charles Kurz's major customers indicated its desire to see one or two large tankers built and made available to meet some of its anticipated transportation needs for the ensuing twenty years. Seeing this as a golden opportunity, Charles Kurz approached the Publickers with a recommendation that they finance the construction of two such "National Defense" tankers. The total expected cost was about $6,000,000. The people at Publickers thought they had better things into which to put money, but their refusal of that offer led to another milestone in the life of Charles Kurz.

Charles then turned to other sources to finance the construction of the first two large tankers he had ever built. Negotiations in New York, which lasted about 30 days, resulted in monetary backing and assured long-term employment for both tankers with Shell Oil Company. Standard Oil Company of New Jersey took a first mortgage at 4-1/2 percent interest for half the delivered cost of the ships, and Irving Trust Company financed one-fourth of the cost with a second mortgage. A new owning company, Keystone Tankship Corporation, was formed, and in 1937 it signed contracts with the Sun Shipbuilding and Dry Dock Company in Chester, Pennsylvania, and the Federal Shipbuilding and Dry Dock Company in Kearny, New Jersey. Each was to construct one ship.

A FAMILY FLEET

For his first tankers to be built and operated independently, Charles Kurz wanted names that would reflect the pride he felt in this accomplishment. Starting with his own initials, "C. K.," he fashioned the name *Seakay* for one, and, using the first three letters of his wife's name, he chose *Markay* for the second. From this there later developed a fleet with related names derived from the names of his three children as well as his sisters Elizabeth and Mary: *Aekay*, *Kalkay*, *Jorkay*, *Ellkay*, and *Emkay*.

The *Seakay* and *Markay*, each at 18,256 tons, were to have twin propellers and unique engines capable of giving them a speed of 18-1/2 knots. No American tanker owners had ever handled vessels with this type of engine. The company's superintending engineer, in spite of abundant experience both in shipbuilding and in the operation of both passenger and dry cargo ships, was unfamiliar with such engines.

The only vessels with similar engines that Charles could find were two passenger ships owned by the Grace Line, the *Santa Paula* and the *Santa Clara*. So it was that I found myself, in November 1938, at the age of 9, on an 18-day Caribbean cruise with my parents aboard the SS *Santa Paula*. I recall sightseeing at the Panama Canal and various island ports, as well as in Venezuela and Columbia. I recall various amusements on the decks of the *Santa Paula*. I even recall my father disappearing into the engine room a few times. But I had no idea of the central purpose of the trip.

Charles Kurz boarded the *Santa Paula* with letters of introduction to the captain and chief engineer from the marine manager of the Grace Line. He not only had permission to learn about the operation of the machinery, but he was told that if he decided to offer anyone a job, simply to be sure to give the Grace Line ample notice.

Charles spent at least three hours every day in the engine room and in discussions with the chief engineer and the first, second, third and fourth assistant. By the end of the voyage, about four engineers had accepted offers to work for Keystone Tankship Corporation, supervising the final construction and installation of machinery and later heading the engine department of the *Seakay* and *Markay* crews. Charles believed that "the marine superintendent of the Grace Line was very pleased,

116

knowing that Keystone would be able to pay the men a better wage."[1]

The Navy, which had had a difficult time finding someone to undertake the high speed tanker project, offered a great deal of help to Charles Kurz in constructing the *Seakay* and the *Markay*. Thus, when the day of the launching finally arrived, Admirals Land and Vickery and other high-ranking Navy and U. S. Maritime Commission officials were present with their wives, as were executives of Shell, Standard Oil, Irving Trust Company, and key employees of the Kurz business. The same day, March 4, 1939, was to see both ships go down the ways. Admiral Vickery's wife smashed the bottle of champagne across the bow of the *Markay* in the morning in northern New Jersey. After that, a private train brought the launching party from nearby Newark to Chester, Pennsylvania, where in the afternoon Mary Kurz did the same to the ship named for her husband.

Undoubtedly the youngest guest at the launching, I climbed the steps to the U-shaped platform into which the bow of the *Seakay* was nuzzled. The railing was brightly decorated in red, white, and blue. The platform was large enough only for a small group of top dignitaries and close family members. The rest had to watch from ground level. My mother was afraid she might miss or fail to break the bottle and thus bring bad luck to the ship.

The bow began to move backwards, perhaps a moment ahead of schedule. Once the ship is free to move, it gains speed rapidly. I think someone reached out to help my mother and almost threw the bottle at the retreating bow. It did break, and horns began to blow on the ship's superstructure, the band played, and shipyard workers, lined along the railing on the ship's deck above us, waved and shouted. The huge hull slid gracefully down the well-greased ways, and within a few minutes was afloat in the middle of the Delaware River. She was soon guided by tugboats to a pier where the launching party was invited to go aboard for a brief inspection. Thereafter the final phases of her construction would be completed.

---

[1]Though he may well have been overestimating the benevolent character of the Grace Line superintendent, many years later Captain Timothy Hayes (see Epilogue), another former Grace Line employee who came to work for Charles Kurz, confirmed that Charles Kurz's account was entirely consistent with the company's policy of "being all for their employees."

16. *Seakay* launching party at Chester, Pennsylvania, March 4, 1939. From left: Beatrice Graves, Kurz's next door neighbor; Mrs. Hazel Griffin; Rudolph Griffin, Shell Oil Company vice president; Mrs. Howard L. Vickery, sponsor of *Markay*; George Kurz; Charles Kurz; Mary Kurz.

118

17. Mary Kurz, sponsor of *Seakay*. Bow of the ship is on the right.

18. *Seakay* gliding down the ways of Sun Shipbuilding and Drydock Company.

The party, banquet, and speeches that followed were a total bore to me. For my father, however, this was the culmination of an enormous amount of planning and work, a singular achievement of his career, and for my mother one of the fullest moments of her life.

The *Seakay* was completed and delivered by the builder on March 23, 1939, and the *Markay* about two months later. A few months later Irving Trust Company advised Charles Kurz of their pleasure with the whole venture and expressed a desire to assume the first mortgage on the ships. Walter Teagle, the president of Standard Oil, had arranged the loan in the first place in order to encourage Charles to pursue this project and in consideration for things he had done in the industry that had been helpful to Standard Oil. Teagle said that Standard Oil was not in the business of financing and would not object to the mortgage being paid off in full. He advised Charles to seek a lower interest rate, such as 2 or 2-1/2 percent. Irving Trust was so happy to get the business that they agreed to take over the first mortgage at 2-1/2 percent.

WARTIME LOSSES AND SERVICE

The optimism of those days was tempered by the onset of World War II. Prior to the war the Kurz group of companies was engaged in a very satisfactory business. Chas. Kurz & Co., Inc., owned five tankers; Paco Tankers, of which Charles Kurz was president, was a wholly-owned subsidiary of Publicker Industries incorporated in December 1936, and owned eleven tankers; and Keystone Tankship Corporation owned the *Markay* and *Seakay*. That was a total of eighteen tankers. In addition, five more National Defense tankers were ordered for construction at the solicitation of the U. S. Maritime Commission and the Navy and had assured long-term employment with responsible parties. Charles Kurz later described those days as "a time when everyone knew his or her job, was content, and hoped not to be drawn into the war." They counted on the ships being able to operate as in normal peacetime and hoped that new ships, yet to be constructed, would be added to the fleet and operated for the duration of their commercial employment contracts.

On October 14, 1940, however, Keystone Tankship Corporation received notice from the Secretary of the Navy that the Navy needed its two ships. Within two weeks the title of the *Seakay* was turned over to the Navy and, on June 24, 1941, the *Markay* likewise became Navy property.

The Navy initially used the *Seakay* and *Markay* as fleet oilers. Later each was converted into an auxiliary aircraft carrier, fitted with a flight deck suitable for the takeoff and landing of small aircraft. As such, they were known as Baby Flattops. Although they reportedly survived the duration of the war, they were never returned to Keystone Tankship Corporation.

The third National Defense tanker to be constructed for Keystone Tankship Corporation was the *Aekay*. In April 1942, just two months after her completion and delivery, the *Aekay* was on a voyage to the Far East when notice of requisition was received; the Navy would take possession of her upon her return to the United States. At the same time, the Navy declared its intention to take over the four other National Defense tankers still being built as soon as their construction was complete.

Countless hours and no end of effort had gone into plans and contracts for construction and for financing of the seven National Defense tankers. But when the last one was completed in September 1942, and taken over by the government the same day, Keystone Tankship Corporation and its affiliated companies, which had been formed to own and operate these tankers, were left with no equipment to operate. Remarkably, replacement tankers for all seven were found, either in the form of new construction or purchase of existing tankers. The government had paid the fair market value of the ships acquired by the Navy, but the time that elapsed between the government's takeover of each ship and the purchase of its replacement combined for a total of 1,543 lost operating days, and hence lost revenue.

During the early years of World War II England and other allied countries suffered serious losses of tankers. On May 1, 1941, seven months prior to the United States entry into the war, Admiral E. S. Land informed industry representatives meeting in Washington that he, as chairman of the U. S. Maritime Commission, had been directed by the President to put twenty-five American tankers at the disposal of the British. The owners reacted anything but favorably to the Admiral's proposal that they release that number of tankers. Admiral Land requested Charles Kurz to take the matter in hand and meet separately with industry representatives that same evening. It was clear that there was no alternative to compliance. The question was how to allocate the burden across the industry.

Meeting at the Willard Hotel, the industry representatives appointed Charles Kurz chairman of a Committee of American Tanker Owners. Deliberations went on until 2 A.M., by which time the majority of owners, including the Kurz group, had committed themselves in writing to withdraw from their commercial trade their pro rata share of 250,000 tons of tankers to aid in the British war effort.

War losses continued. The need for oil became more acute. Calls for additional tankers, including requirements of the Russians, came through Admiral Land and later through Interior Secretary Ickes. They were handled similarly by Kurz and his committee.

In the midst of an acute shortage of tankers, the government had in lay-up several foreign flag tankers, which, because they belonged to unfriendly nations, had been seized early in the war. Some were in deplorable condition and would require major overhaul before they could be put in service. Ship owners generally wanted nothing to do with such interned ships, and Charles Kurz was advised to avoid them.

The Maritime Commission nevertheless persuaded Kurz to take on the task that other tanker operators had declined, that of putting three of these tankers in operation. Everyone concerned recognized the danger that operating such vessels could jeopardize American flag ships. A hostile country might seize an American ship in retaliation. Consultations in Washington led to a plan to put the three tankers under the Panamanian flag and keep their operation separate from that of the Kurz group. A new corporation, Keystone Shipping Company,[2] was thus organized to manage the repair and operation of these three foreign ships under a general agency contract with the government.

When the United States entered World War II in December 1941, all remaining ships belonging to the Kurz companies were "requisitioned" by the government. Under a service agreement with the War Shipping Administration, Keystone Shipping

---

[2]Incorporated on June 26, 1941.

Company was made responsible for all aspects of the operation of these vessels. Construction of new tankers for the Maritime Commission was ordered on a large scale. Kurz was advised to gear up his organization to operate about seventy-five tankers under the service agreement. The number of tankers allocated to Keystone Shipping Company increased. By April 1944, virtually all personnel in the Kurz group of companies were transferred to Keystone Shipping Company.

The U. S. Government also asked Charles Kurz to examine a "T-2" tanker, known as the *White Plains*, that was being built at Sun Shipyard for the U. S. Maritime Commission. She had been allocated to another company for operation, but they had refused to accept her, claiming that it would be very risky to operate a tanker with a spar deck such as she had where landing barges, jeeps, and other military equipment would be carried.

So Kurz, along with a group of associates, went to Chester to inspect the ship. They agreed to accept allocation of the *White Plains* to Keystone Shipping Company. She became the first T-2 tanker to sail with her tanks below deck carrying oil and a spar deck loaded with landing craft, military airplanes, and other equipment necessary for the Armed Forces. Successful voyages by the *White Plains* convinced others of the feasibility of such an operation, and the spar deck with military equipment became commonplace.

Kurz was responsible for numerous other innovations during those years, such as allowing the load line, which had been fixed by International Convention, to be modified to an "emergency load line." That is, tankers could be more fully loaded. Foreign flag tankers could be used for coastwise domestic trade.[3] Tanker speed could be increased. The routine dry docking of tankers every eight months could be deferred where possible. All of these had the effect of increasing tanker tonnage available for military and commercial needs.

In addition, Kurz encouraged the further development of the U. S. Merchant Marine Cadet Corps and led the way in employing such cadets on tankers. He recommended a training

---

[3] A term used for transportation of cargo from one United States port to another. This is normally restricted to American flag tankers.

program for licensed engineers and other personnel needed to man the T-2 tankers that the government was building.

In recognition of his service to his country in time of war, Charles Kurz received, in November 1946, a distinctive letter of commendation from the Chief of Naval Operations, Fleet Admiral Chester W. Nimitz (Appendix A). That letter remains proudly displayed on the wall of his study.

Chapter 14

TO STRIKE A GOOD DEAL

While Charles Kurz was involved with developing a fleet of tankers, he was also looking to broaden the uses of Pier 70. The presence of a railroad siding with facilities for ten freight cars next to Pier 70 North suggested possible uses for the pier in addition to storing and transporting salt. One idea that Charles successfully implemented was the manufacture of cinder blocks and concrete blocks for the construction industry. The gravel and other materials were brought in by rail, then hauled from the track onto the pier. The machines that produced the blocks were right on the pier.

But Charles Kurz was not the only one dreaming up ideas to utilize Pier 70. In the early 1920s, there was a lot of activity from the pier. For example, motor trucks went out from there regularly loaded with salt for Breyer's Ice Cream Company and several large dairies, like Supplee, that also made ice cream.

MINDING HIS OWN BUSINESS

One day Kurz was approached by a group of smartly dressed men who told him they could keep that pier even busier. They wanted to use his trucks to transport a commodity they did not wish to identify. Though skeptical, Kurz offered to show them around the pier, but they replied that they already knew it—and knew as well that it was just the ideal place to conduct their business, utilizing Kurz's trucks to transport their goods. Charles invited them into his little office on the pier, and they proceeded to make him a fabulous offer; and they even were willing to pay cash. After some discussion, however, their plan finally came out. They intended to have liquor brought by lighter from import ships to Pier 70. The lighters would be unloaded by night when no one would be around. Then, during the day, they would put a certain number of cases of liquor on each truck, cover them over with salt, and proceed as if on normal deliveries to Breyers and the dairies.

Since most of the trucks did not actually belong to the Kurz company (teamsters handled a good part of the hauling), Kurz suggested that they would have to buy the trucks or provide their own.

The men were obviously shrewd and not new to this kind of operation. Charles realized later that Philadelphia was only one of many U. S. ports where they were involved in bootlegging. They knew all the tricks. As they talked, he began to get the feeling that if something went wrong, Charles Kurz could easily be the one to wind up in jail. He could lose everything—the salt business, the jobs it provided for people he cared about.

So Charles thanked them very much but told them he would not be interested in their proposal. Charles Kurz always suspected that his visitors were heavy contributors to the political party in power, for, to his knowledge, none of them ever wound up in jail.

Although he refused that fabulous offer, Charles Kurz's business continued to grow. By the late 1920s, the need for expanded office space became pressing. In May 1929, less than a month after the incorporation of the Pennsylvania Shipping Company, Charles moved his offices to larger quarters in the Atlantic Building.

When the stock market crashed later that year, Charles's interests remained stable. He had friends who lost everything. Widows lost their homes. Stockbrokers committed suicide. Everybody was down and out. "But while they were losing," Charles Kurz recalls, "I was progressing." As he saw it, "I was minding my own business." He didn't have any large stock investments to lose because "I couldn't afford to invest in these things where people thought they could get rich overnight."

He did, however, buy some gold mine stocks. "Put your money into gold," Walter Winchell told people over the radio, and people, including Charles Kurz, regarded him as an authority. So Charles bought about $400 worth of stock in a gold mine in

Colorado, and he still has that stock today. However, it never pays a dividend, and it still isn't worth any more than $400.

LABOR NEGOTIATIONS

In shipping, as in other industries during the 1930s, labor was steadily becoming better organized and the need to negotiate ever more pressing. For years the American Steamship Owners' Association had fought off all efforts on the part of seamen to bargain collectively. According to a newspaper story[1] in 1934, the ship owners' statements usually professed a willingness to bargain; yet organized labor was consistently met with the argument that it did not represent all shipping labor. There could, therefore, be no collective bargaining. At the same time, however, ship owners were issuing handouts to the press urging more and bigger government subsidies for American shipping. Thus, in a Pacific Coast ship workers' strike, "The owners were brought to heel only by means of the government's subsidy whip."

Charles Kurz was all too familiar with the violence that so readily accompanied shipping strikes. On one occasion when two Pennsylvania Shipping Company employees attempted to go to one of his ships that was tied up by a work stoppage, they were stopped at the picket line, interrogated, and beaten up. Both wound up hospitalized with broken legs. Charles always suspected that such action took place with the full knowledge and encouragement of the powers in Washington.

Nevertheless, Charles Kurz was confident that ship owners and employees could sit down and work out a mutually acceptable agreement. It was Robert L. Hague, president of Standard Oil's shipping subsidiary, who was the first to recognize the Seafarers' Council (formed in the spring of 1934). He urged the other members of the relatively progressive tanker owners group to do likewise. The tanker group attempted to get the full membership of the Steamship Owners' Association to consent to collective bargaining. On meeting the usual petty objections, it decided to proceed independently.

On the insistence of Hague, Charles Kurz took the responsibility for leading a special committee of the tanker division of the owners to negotiate in New York with the Seafarers' Coun-

---

[1]*Philadelphia Record*, August 20, 1934.

cil. The tanker group itself lacked unanimity, and some members held out against any negotiations. The tanker owners had five representatives at the conference table, including Charles Kurz and Captain Mathiasen, both from Pennsylvania Shipping Company; while the seven Seafarers' Council representatives were drawn from member labor organizations such as United Licensed Officers, Radio Telegraphers' Association, Marine Cooks' and Stewards' Union, Marine Firemen, Oilers' and Watertenders' Union, and Atlantic Gulf Sailors' Association.

The resulting agreement, reached in August 1934, was hailed by the press as the first wage pact between ship workers and operators in twelve years. The agreement affected some 13,000 officers and crew members of more than 362 tankers.

Charles Kurz was reported to have "presided at round table discussions," which he described as harmonious at all times. To him, they confirmed what he had held from the beginning— that a final agreement satisfactory to both sides could be reached. The agreement included wage increases of 10 to 20 percent, fixed wage scales, an eight-hour work day, 14-day vacations for officers, and an annual seven-day vacation for unlicensed personnel. Bert L. Todd, vice-president of the Council, hailed the agreement as a "fine start." Charles Kurz remembers it this way:

"I was the arbitrator. I met with the union from nine o'clock in the morning until five o'clock in the afternoon. And they all protested that. They wanted to start at 7 P.M. But all they would do is get together for an hour, then go out to eat, and then drink and drink and drink. Then they wouldn't know what the hell they were talking about. They would just dilly dally along and never come to an agreement."

"But I insisted on two things: negotiations must begin at 9 A.M. and during the negotiations there could be no interference with employment on any ships."

Each morning, for thirty days, Charles took the 7 A.M. Reading train from Philadelphia and walked from the ferry landing at the foot of Liberty Street to 7 Battery Place, where the arbitration meetings were held. At quarter to five he closed up and headed for the ferry and the train back to Philadelphia. The whole way there and back, he worked. He and Captain Mathiasen usually had a drawing room on the train where there was privacy to study the material to be discussed at the next negotiating session. Mr. Foy or Mr. Dieterle, two of Kurz's stenographers, rode along with them to take dictation and type reports. They arrived each morning fully prepared to go right to business.

After about 30 days, the group of negotiators arrived at a decision that pleased all the labor leaders present. Charles was also very pleased. It was submitted to a general meeting of the tanker owners group the following morning and unanimously approved. The press report, referring to the previous holdouts among the tanker owners, stated, "Upon adoption of the present successful agreement, all have agreed to stand by it."

After the meeting as Charles was walking down Broadway with one of the important labor leaders, he said, "Mr. Kurz, you mean to tell me you rode to New York every morning and back to Philadelphia every night while these negotiations were going on?"

"Yes, sir. I've been doing that for thirty days," Charles replied.

"Well, you're a wonderful fellow. And you accomplished something that most every arbitrator wasn't able to do. Now, why couldn't you have an office in New York?"

"I don't want to have an office in New York, and I'd rather not stay in New York overnight. I probably wouldn't get anything constructive accomplished that way."

Reaching that labor-management accord was undoubtedly the most noteworthy achievement of Charles Kurz's career to that point. From then on he served as a member of the Executive Committee of the American Steamship Owners' Association. In June 1938, when it became the American Merchant Marine Institute, he remained on that board as well, and in 1942 he organized its Tanker Committee. He served continuously as chairman of that committee from its inception on October 8, 1942, until his resignation in December 1964 (see Appendix B).

Chapter 15

LOSS AND GROWTH

By the end of World War II, the Kurz group of companies had lost four old ships and one new one to enemy action. The old tankers—two belonging to Chas. Kurz & Co., Inc., the *Naeco* and the *Camden*, and two belonging to Paco Tankers, Inc., the *Hagen* and the *Meton*—ranged from twenty-one to twenty-four years old when they were lost in 1942. Not surprisingly, they were small ships. The *Meton*, at 10,710 tons, was the largest, and the *Naeco*, at 8,649 tons, was the smallest. The new ship that was lost, however, was a 16,550-ton tanker, a second *Seakay* that was built to replace the original. In March 1944, only one and a half years after her completion, the second *Seakay* was sunk by a German submarine near the coast of England. Remarkably, the captain, A. K. Jorgenson, and the entire crew got off before the ship went down, and all were rescued.

The burdens of World War II—including the five ships lost to enemy action, frequent trips to Washington and New York, difficult negotiations with government and industry leaders, and work hours that more often than not extended late into the night and included Saturdays, Sundays, and holidays—eventually took their toll. Charles Kurz was told by his doctor that he must slow down. He was instructed to leave his office at three o'clock in the afternoon and go out to play golf in the fresh air. To Charles Kurz, a doctor's orders, like those of a ship captain, were to be obeyed.

Thus he instituted a major change in lifestyle. He indeed came home at three o'clock several times a week and took Mary out to play nine holes of golf. After supper, however, he returned to his desk on the sun porch and began work on the papers he had stuffed into his bulging briefcase. At the office he could keep multiple secretaries busy taking dictation and doing his typing, but at home he did his own typing. He prided himself on maintaining that skill, which he had learned more than forty years previously under the guidance of Russell Conwell and his instructors at Temple. To this day, an electric typewriter sitting on its stand next to his desk still gets ample use, although to Charles Kurz it "doesn't spell as well as the manual ones used to."

THE MARKAY DISASTER

Even more stressful for Charles than the events of wartime, was an event that occurred nearly two years after V-J Day, in June 1947. The second *Markay* was a 16,550-ton tanker that had been built at Sun Shipyard and delivered on October 13, 1942. She was a sister ship to the second *Seakay*. To Charles, she was "a beautiful ship and one of the most up-to-date then in existence." He had "worked like hell to work the thing out so we could buy it." The Irving Trust Company gladly financed it at about 1-1/2 percent for 20 years. The ship was just newly back in commercial service after the war and under a long-term contract with Shell Oil Company.

The *Markay* was in port at the Shell dock on Mormon Island, a peninsula at Wilmington, California, when she suffered an explosion. It was suspected that someone might have tossed a lit cigarette out a porthole, thus igniting the high octane gasoline that she carried. There was one explosion after another. Fortunately, most of the crew was ashore, but everyone in the midship house was killed—five or six men, including Captain Karl Hogstrum, one of Kurz's best port captains. In addition, the physical damage to the *Markay* was so extensive that she had to be declared a total loss.

According to newspaper accounts of the incident,[1,2] a series of three tremendous blasts that rocked Los Angeles Harbor began aboard the *Markay* at 2:05 A.M. on June 22, 1947. Eyewitnesses said the ship was immediately enveloped in flames that shot high in the sky and provided daylight brightness. Windows were shattered at a store nearly five miles away.

---

[1]*New York Times*, June 23, 1947, pp. 1 and 3.

[2]*Los Angeles Times*, June 23, 1947, pp. 1 and 2; June 24, 1947, pp. 1 and 2.

Several crew members climbed hand over hand down the mooring lines to the pier. Others jumped from the deck into the water. Some made it to safety. Others perished in the heat and smoke on the ship or in the flaming fuel on the surface of the water. A Catholic Priest, who was hurled from his bed in San Pedro more than a mile away by the terrific blast, told of rescuing two men who were struggling in the water. The dazed men had swum nearly a mile down the main channel of Los Angeles Harbor in a fearful race against the pursuing flames.

The loading berths where the *Markay* was docked were destroyed. A half-ton piece of the ship's hull was blown more than 1,000 feet over the Shell terminal into an unoccupied Texas Company office. Docks leased to the American President Lines, also about 1,000 feet away, were gutted and twisted into shambles.

Fourteen Los Angeles fire companies joined five harbor companies, three city fire boats, and Navy and Coast Guard fire boats in battling the rivers of fire that spread over the harbor waters. Heroic efforts prevented the flames from spreading to an adjacent "oil farm" where 16,000,000 gallons more of petroleum products were stored in twenty huge tanks.

The fire raged for five hours before it was declared under control, leaving total damages estimated at $10,000,000, according to the same reports.

The *Markay*, which had been loading a mixed cargo of aviation gasoline, automotive gasoline, stove oil, and diesel fuel, was reduced to a smoldering hulk and lay on the bottom in the shape of an open V, nearly broken in two. Her bow and stern angled crazily out of the harbor waters. The *Markay* was surveyed by the salvage associations on behalf of the underwriters on June 24 and, based on the opinions that she could not be repaired, was declared a "constructive total loss" on June 25, 1947.

According to Charles's son, Adolph, although there were numerous speculations, the precise cause of the disaster could not be determined. The most plausible theory was that gas accumulated under the midship house where switches were not explosion-proof.

FINDING A REPLACEMENT

That explosion on the other side of the continent shook Charles Kurz to the core. "I was terribly upset," he recounted. "You're a young guy and you start things and think you're somebody big. You go to bed feeling swell and you wake up in the morning to find you've got nothing. The loss of the *Markay* affected me personally, and my doctor ordered me not to travel, to take it easy."

But Charles wouldn't stop there. He had to find a replacement as similar to the *Markay* as possible in order to fulfill his contract with Shell. Among the many ships that the U. S. Maritime Commission had in lay-up was a T-2 tanker named *Catawba Ford*. Following his doctor's advice, he did stay in Philadelphia and sent Fred Perdum to Washington to advise the Commission of the *Markay*'s misfortune and to seek charter or . purchase of a suitable replacement from the government, such as the *Catawba Ford*.

Perdum reported to his boss daily. None of the potential buyers of government ships were getting satisfactory answers to their questions as to price or conditions or even whether the Commission had authority to sell them. After about thirty days, Kurz gave Perdum a deadline of two more days in which to get results. The following morning Kurz received a ten-page letter that Perdum had drafted to be sent to each member of the Commission over Charles Kurz's signature. But Charles concluded that the letter was too nasty and that it would do more harm than good. He ordered Perdum home. Much as he disliked doing so, Charles decided to go to Washington and handle the job himself.

The general counsel for the Maritime Commission, Wade Skinner, was an old business acquaintance who agreed to meet Kurz in Washington. Over breakfast the next morning, Charles explained the reasons why his desire to purchase the *Catawba Ford* should receive top priority. The Commission, he was told, having no money in its budget, could not pay for the repairs that were essential to put these ships in class (in safe operating condition and able to pass an insurance inspection), as required by law. Therefore no ships could be sold until Congress appropriated sufficient money to the Commission.

As Charles understood it, the law did not specify where the money to put the ships in class had to come from. So he suggested that they sell him the *Catawba Ford*; that the Commission's Maintenance and Repair Department cooperate with his superintendent of repairs to develop specifications to be submitted to various shipyards for bids; that the Commission award the repair job to the lowest bidder; and that he would pay the repair bill and deduct it from the purchase price of the ship.

Skinner was amazed that no one else had thought of such a simple solution, but he warned Charles Kurz the government might take unfair advantage of him. Confident that a contract could be written with adequate safeguards, Kurz said he was willing to take the risk. The Commission was scheduled to meet at 9:15 A.M. that very day. The attorney took Kurz to his office and he waited there while the Commission considered his proposal. In about twenty minutes the general counsel came out and announced: "The ship is yours!"

Within two days all details of the contract were settled, and steps were initiated to get the ship ready. Charles Kurz's plan became a model that the Commission used in selling additional ships, while avoiding the necessity of a congressional appropriation. The *Catawba Ford* was put in class at government expense, and title passed to the Keystone Tankship Corporation on August 25, 1947.

Nevertheless, the *Markay* explosion gave Charles Kurz many sleepless nights. An expression he used repeatedly, "You worry your soulcase out," reflected his feelings about that incident more than any other in his life. A year later he applied for a large amount of life insurance. The rating given as a result of his medical examination required that premiums be higher than the already high premiums expected for a man of sixty. At that time he was thought to have heart disease, symptoms of angina, and less than a normal life expectancy. If Charles Kurz had a mid-life crisis, this was it—it had simply been postponed until the war was over and occurred in his late fifties instead of the age to which we have grown accustomed nowadays.

NEW SHIPS, NEW COMPANIES

The doctors who made their dire predictions about his longevity, to my knowledge, have all died, but Charles Kurz recovered. Within a few years more new ships were on the ways at other shipyards. For example, 1953 saw the launching of two 18,000-ton ships, the SS *Keytanker* and the SS *Keystoner*, and the following year the SS *Keytrader*, all at Bethlehem-Sparrows Point Shipyard in Sparrows Point, Maryland, all for Keystone

Tankship Corporation. In 1955, the SS *Mobilgas*, built for Chas. Kurz & Co., Inc., was launched by the Bethlehem Steel Company's Shipbuilding Division in Quincy, Massachusetts. The SS *Philine*, largest ship of its type ever constructed by the New York Shipbuilding Corporation, slid down its Camden, New Jersey, ways in October 1958, to be followed the next year by sister ships *Phillipia* and *Philidora*. Those three were chartered by Asiatic Petroleum Corporation, one of the companies of the Royal Dutch Shell group. In a shipyard as far away as Mitsubishi Shipbuilding & Engineering Co., Ltd. in Nagasaki, Japan, two 45,000-ton tankers, the *Kenai Peninsula* and the *Cuyama Valley*, were built in 1958 for charter to Richfield Oil Company.

Faced with the lower cost of transportation of molasses from Cuba by foreign flag competitors, Charles Kurz devised a plan to utilize three American flag tankers belonging to Paco Tankers, Inc. As President of Paco, Kurz obtained transfer rights from the U. S. Maritime Administration and authorization to proceed with his plan from S. S. Neuman, President of Publicker Industries, Inc., which owned Paco. Accordingly, the *Kittanning*, the *Petersburg*, and the *Fredericksburg* (named for a town in Pennsylvania and two Civil War battlefields in Virginia) were placed under Liberian flag and renamed the *Lyric*, the *Aldine*, and the *Palace* (all movie theaters in Philadelphia). Their ownership was transferred to a subsidiary of Paco organized for this purpose and incorporated in Monrovia, Liberia, on December 21, 1953. It was appropriately named Theatre Navigation Corporation. Less than seven years later, however, market conditions required the lay-up of the three floating theaters, and Theatre Navigation Corporation ceased doing business in the fall of 1960.

Two years later a long, and sometimes stormy, association grew to a close when Charles Kurz resigned from his position as vice-president of Publicker Industries, Inc., over differences with that company's new leadership. He had held that position from May 1929 until August 1962. The Pennsylvania Shipping Company, originally formed in May 1929 to operate ships for Publickers, was dissolved in December 1963. Charles Kurz had been its president during its entire history.

During the 1960s, Keystone Shipping Company was the principal operating company for the Kurz tanker fleet. For example, in July 1964, Keystone Shipping Company operated three ships owned by Paco, eight owned by Chas. Kurz & Co., Inc., eight

138

owned by Keystone Tankship Corporation, six by the Military Sea Transportation Co., Inc., and two owned by itself, for a total of twenty-seven ships.

Numerous new companies were formed in the 1950s and 1960s and on into the 1970s. Some took older ships, enlarged them, and chartered them for service to various oil companies. The *David E. Day*, for example, was an American flag 16,500-ton T-2 tanker that was "jumboized" at Todd's Shipyard in San Pedro, California, in 1958. Stated simply, she was cut in half, and a new section was inserted between the forward and after portions. This remarkable procedure, which increased her deadweight tonnage to approximately 20,000, took only about two months. Locust Tankers, Inc., which had been formed for the sole purpose of owning this ship, then chartered her to Richfield for a fifteen-year period of service.

The largest ships of the Keystone fleet, the *Atigun Pass* and the *Keystone Canyon*, were built in 1977 at Avondale Shipyards in New Orleans. Each has a staggering deadweight tonnage of 173,619, more than ten times that of the second *Seakay* and *Markay*.

Although the word "tanker" became nearly synonymous with "oil tanker," and indeed the majority of the Kurz ships still transport petroleum products, new uses for tankers have developed in the past three decades that were unimagined before World War II. Tankers now carry a wide range of liquid chemicals, requiring specialized cargo containment and pumping systems and new techniques for safe handling of such products. Among them are acetic acid, anhydrous ammonia, benzene, caustic soda, methanol, napthalene and phenol.

The most significant new cargo for tankers has been grain. Wheat and other grains can be loaded from a grain elevator through chutes into tanks to be carried in bulk and removed from the tanks with agricultural vacuvators. In the mid-1950s, Kurz ships began carrying surplus wheat, rye, and barley to areas of shortage such as Bangladesh, Korea, Greece, India, and Pakistan for the governments of those countries. Charles Kurz recalls that the *Pine Ridge* was the first tanker of the Keystone fleet to take a cargo of barley to Europe, and that was in April 1956. Later, Keystone vessels were among the first to transport grain to the Soviet Union. More recently, Kurz tankers have carried natural gas, which is liquefied by cooling it to $-240°$ F.

139

The most recent Keystone innovation is a ship to carry coal in bulk from Atlantic Coast ports to New England Electric generating plants in Massachusetts. This 36,000-ton capacity ship, constructed in Quincy, Massachusetts, was completed in the spring of 1983. She is owned jointly by New England Electric and Keystone Shipping Company and is operated by the latter. She is expected to transport 2.2 million tons of coal to New England a year, enough to replace 9 million barrels of foreign oil. This ship not only carries coal, but is powered by coal as well.

NEW QUARTERS

As the size and activities of Kurz's fleets multiplied over the years, Charles Kurz's business quarters also changed and grew. By May 1929, he had already moved his office out of Pier 70 North. For many years thereafter the Atlantic Building on the northwest corner of Broad and Spruce Streets was the site of the principal offices of the Kurz companies. This was an ideal location from the standpoint of public transportation, for at that corner was an entrance to the Broad Street subway from which Charles Kurz could ride to the northern end of the line, then at Broad and Olney, in about twenty minutes. From there to home was a matter of less that ten minutes by car. In September 1946, the organization moved to the Jefferson Building at 1015 Chestnut Street, renting office space that had just been vacated by the Eastern Regional Office of the U. S. Maritime Commission. The Jefferson Building was likewise convenient to public transportation. It was an easy walk to Reading Terminal at 12th and Market, a twenty or twenty-five minute train ride to Fern Rock Station on Godfrey Avenue, and less than five minutes by car from there to home.

In 1950, faced with rising rents and a critical need for additional space, Charles Kurz decided to buy his own building. The Western Saving Fund Society of Philadelphia had relocated its main office and wished to sell its previous principal banking location on the southwest corner of 10th and Walnut Streets. The building had impressive columns surrounding its entrances on Walnut Street, extremely high ceilings, and far more floor space than his organization required. With appropriate renovation, part of the second floor could be rented out. Moreover, there was a small parking lot adjacent to the building, just right for employees who drove to work. Charles was convinced that the Western Saving Fund building would be an ideal permanent location for his main office. The building was purchased, renovations were completed, and the organization moved to 1000 Walnut Street in August 1950. Charles was justifiably proud of his new office. It met his expectations and he anticipated that it would serve his companies' needs for years to come.

One day, not many months after this relocation, Charles Kurz was working late into the evening. His new office was in the far southwest corner of the building diagonally opposite the main entrance, and could be reached only after passing through a maze of narrow corridors which ran between partitions just high enough to prevent one from seeing into the offices on either side and several swinging doors. Nearly everyone else had gone home when suddenly a man appeared in Charles's office and approached his desk. "I thought at first he was a holdup man," Charles recalls, "but then he started to show me his bank book. He had an old savings account passbook in which he had made a deposit fifteen or twenty years previously, in a day when the bank had been open at night to accommodate working people. He was back to make another deposit."

When asked why there had been no other transactions in all those years, the man explained that he had been away from Philadelphia and didn't know transactions could be made by mail. Charles realized that the exterior of the building still looked like a bank and, with the inside all lit up, the man just looked around until he found someone to talk to.

"I did a little figuring on the interest," Charles recounted, "compounded over those years, and came up with an approximate balance. I don't recall just how much, but it seemed like a lot of money at that time. When I mentioned the interest they would be adding to his passbook, he grew wide-eyed and thanked me. I told my visitor that his bank had moved to Broad and Chestnut, but they were not open evenings."

The day came, however, when Keystone Shipping also had to do its business elsewhere; the city of Philadelphia required the building at 10th and Walnut for an expansion of the Thomas Jefferson University. In December 1966 the Kurz organization again purchased and renovated a building to serve as its principal office. The location at 313 Chestnut Street, less than two blocks from the site of the old Drexel Building where Charles Kurz started to work for S. G. Simpson sixty-five years earlier, remains the headquarters of Keystone Shipping Company to this day.

RECOGNITION

Thirty years ago, as part of a brief personal sketch, Charles Kurz wrote the following summary of the work of the Kurz companies:

> The organization provides a world-wide shipping service by ocean-going tankers, specializing in the transportation of petroleum products and other liquids, such as molasses, chemicals, vegetable oils, tallow, and fish oils.
>
> The operation of these tankers includes the supervision while they are built, securing of charters for employment of the tankers, issuing of instructions for operation, the manning, victualling, drydocking and repairing, and accounting necessary to keep the vessels profitably employed.
>
> At times, the organization charters ships of others to transport cargoes for account of customers.
>
> The organization also acts as agent for several dry cargo steamship companies.

Keystone, he could now add, also has provided consultative services to other companies for construction and management of their ships. For example, Keystone is ship construction advisor to Pacific Lighting Company for a vessel to carry liquefied natural gas.

Charles Kurz's own factual summary of his companies' functions does not convey either the full magnitude of his activities or the impact that they had on the growth of American shipping in the twentieth century. However, his leadership role was widely recognized by his colleagues and counterparts as well as many government officials. The 1962 Maritime Man of the Year award gave public recognition to the role he had already played for decades, and Vice President Lyndon Johnson, making the presentation at the Capitol, commented that even at that time the award was long overdue. The congratulatory letters that flooded Charles Kurz (some of which are reproduced in Appendix C) testify to the respect he had earned not only for his enormous business success but, more importantly, for the time, effort, and resources that he devoted to serving the industry and his government as well.

Despite the proclamation and ceremonies in Washington, Charles Kurz was nonetheless surprised when, one day later that year, he entered a taxi at 30th Street Station in Philadelphia and was recognized by the driver. The driver turned and asked if his passenger knew him, but Charles did not recall the man.

"Your name is Kurz, isn't it?" the driver asked.

"Yes," he replied. "How do you know me?"

"Oh! I remember you well from Temple Night School. I was in the same class with you, only you were always at the head of the class, and I was usually at the bottom. I've often wondered what became of you."

Charles told him that he had been very lucky to have an office job where he could put into practice what he learned at Temple. "My bosses were lazy," Charles explained, "so I had more opportunities to do things and learn than most young men and that's how I could advance. Now I have my own business," he said simply.

That statement seems to summarize the view that Charles Kurz must have developed early in life. For him, the world was full of opportunities, all sorts of possibilities just waiting to be grasped. All that one needs, he always believed, is the imagination to see the possibilities and a lot of hard work to turn them into realities.

For him it was also a world full of good people who were anxious to help a promising young person to succeed. "Oh, there are a few who may try to do you in," he would say, "but don't waste time worrying about them." He didn't.

Chapter 16

LATER YEARS

The marriage of Mary Breuninger and Charles Kurz came to a close on September 21, 1962, just three months prior to their 50th anniversary, when Mary fell victim to heart disease. She was seventy-two. The following day the family gathered on the sun porch of the home on 6th Street with Richard Armstrong, minister of the Oak Lane Presbyterian Church, so that he might gain insights into the life of Mary B. Kurz in order to prepare his funeral message. Armstrong's history with that church was short in comparison with Mary Kurz's active participation for over thirty years.

The pastor asked her husband and her sons to state in turn what kind of person she had been and what her life had meant to each of them. Thus he became a catalyst for the family to put into words, in front of him and each other, what they felt about their wife and mother. The therapeutic effect was profound.

With a slow, laboured gait, Charles Kurz climbed the twenty-seven steps to the mausoleum behind the casket bearing his wife to her final resting place. There was none of his usual bounce. Yet he showed his grief in no other way and appeared to cope with remarkable equanimity, as he had throughout his life, accepting the disappointments along with the joys and successes. Immediately he took up the problem of settling Mary's estate, a task made complex by the fact that he had never anticipated it. He had developed an estate plan on the assumption that his doctors were right—that he was the one with the shorter life expectancy.

Business matters occupied much of Charles's time in the following year when he continued living in the house in Oak Lane. Helen and Jack Jarrells, his household employees, lived on the third floor of the home. During the last years of Mary Kurz's life, when her health seriously failed, they had cared for her devotedly; after her death, their loyalty continued, and they provided much support for Charles Kurz in his bereavement.

A weekly routine soon developed that came to symbolize Charles's devotion to Mary. After Sunday morning worship at the Oak Lane Presbyterian Church, Jack would drive him to the Chelten Hills Abbey, where he climbed the same mausoleum steps and stood before the crypt in remembrance of his wife.

At the time of Mary's death, the Oak Lane Presbyterian Church was embarking on a fund-raising campaign for renovations. The most notable need was in the church basement, about one-third of which had never been fully excavated. The dirt floor in this area gradually rose toward the north end of the building. The space was useless for anything but storage.

Charles determined that Mary's death notice in the Philadelphia *Bulletin* specified: "In lieu of flowers, contributions may be made to the Oak Lane Presbyterian Church Renovation Fund." Then soon after the funeral, his friend and personal physician, Dr. Alfred E. Krick, persuaded Charles to do something significant as a memorial to his wife. Dr. Krick happened to be chairman of the church's building committee. Today the north end of the basement has been excavated, and it now contains a hallway, nursery, lavatories and utility room. Major improvements have also been made in the other section of the basement, the pastor's study, and various rooms in the Sunday School area. Yet, despite the fact that both the current pastor, David Thompson, and trustee John Fowler[1] know that Charles Kurz was a major contributor to the renovation fund, no plaque is to be found. In the church's "Book of Remembrances," one finds records of 89 gifts totaling $4,070 to the Renovation Fund made between September 1962 and December 1963 in memory of Mary B. Kurz from persons who had heeded the request in the newspaper obituary. But the name of Charles Kurz is not to be found among the donors.

"I'm not surprised," Rev. Thompson has commented. "That's true to his character."

In addition to his support for churches, Charles Kurz has been

---

[1]The two men with whom I spoke on a visit to the church nineteen years after my mother's death.

a generous supporter of educational, medical, and other charitable institutions over the years. With his contributions, he has consistently insisted on anonymity. A recurring paragraph in letters transmitting his gifts reads: "It is my policy to avoid publicity and I request that you make no public announcement, and do not install a plaque or any other evidence of this or any future gift which I may decide to make."

Exactly one year after Mary's death, Charles received an unexpected letter from Richard Armstrong. It contained words of affirmation and inspiration that brought comfort on a difficult anniversary. Charles saved that letter, and it is reproduced in Appendix D.

REMARRIAGE

Charles was in no rush to remarry. Once having made his decision, however, he let no grass grow under his feet. From the time he gave the first hint that he was considering remarriage until he and Anne T. Moran said their vows on March 14, 1964, no more than three weeks elapsed. Anne, then fifty-seven years old, had been a key member of his secretarial staff for some twenty-two years. During that time she developed, as did the other members of his staff, great respect, admiration, loyalty, and love for him. Not only did she know him well, but she also had known Mary and the rest of the family.

Anne and Charles lived in the home on 6th Street for a time, but the house was too large for them. When Helen Jarrells became ill and could no longer continue her job, the likelihood of finding a new couple of the high caliber of Jack and Helen seemed remote. The prospect of Anne being alone in that big house disturbed Charles and led to a decision to leave the place he had called home for over forty years. In December 1965 the house was sold, and Anne and Charles took up their present residence in a Center City apartment.

The ritual of Sunday visits to the cemetery continued whenever Anne and Charles were not out of town. After Jack Jarrells was no longer available to do the driving, Charles's car was driven by a hired chauffeur. Anne, who was devoted both to Charles and to the memory of Mary, regularly accompanied him on his pilgrimage. Not until about ten years after Mary's death, when Charles's legs no longer could climb the mausoleum steps, did the visits cease.

147

Anne described Mary as "kindness itself," a woman who "would get food out of the freezer to give to poor people who came begging at the door." When Mary died, Anne had been among the few members of his secretarial staff whom Charles personally invited to the funeral.

During the first ten years of their marriage, Anne and Charles were able to do many things together, including winter trips to Florida, occasional summer days in Atlantic City, and frequent Sunday lunches with son George and his family in Flemington, New Jersey. They even attempted a Caribbean cruise on the *Europa* in 1973. On board ship, however, Charles suffered a fall while attempting to navigate a doorway, and the cruise had to be cut short. A fracture of the left side of the pelvis was diagnosed, and Charles spent a total of thirty days in hospitals. Later that same year a second fall occurred. This time it was in the hallway of a hotel in Atlantic City, and the right side of his pelvis had a hairline fracture. He was hospitalized again for eighteen days. The first fall hadn't stopped him, and at age eighty-five the second fall didn't stop him either.

On September 29, 1977, Charles Kurz was hospitalized with acute pain all over his body. Examinations and tests over a period of a week failed to pinpoint the cause, and his condition rapidly deteriorated. By Sunday, October 9, he was semi-comatose, had to be restrained, and was intermittently struggling to get up and call a taxi to go to his office.

That evening Anne and his children left the hospital convinced that he would not survive another 24 hours. But, to the amazement of everyone, the next day he bagan to improve. He was soon fully alert and able to sit up and feed himself. A week later, he had regained much of his strength and was in a talkative mood.

Charles Kurz was discharged from the hospital and returned to his apartment on October 22. Up until that illness, he had continued going to his office, even though only for a few hours each morning. Now, at eighty-nine, his strength was severely diminished. No one expected him to return to the office, but on April 8, 1978, he did just that, and he continued going right through his 90th birthday.

After July 10, 1978, however, his physical presence was no longer to be seen at Keystone Shipping company. Nevertheless, messengers continued to bring volumes of desk work for him to do at home. The routine of mail pickup and delivery three times a day continued for several more years and allowed him to remain active. At ninety-four years of age, he remained fully aware of activities in his business as well as the industry in general. Although active management of Keystone Shipping Company has been in the hands of his sons Adolph and Karl, major business decisions have been made only after consultation with Charles Kurz. Only in the absence of deception, do Adolph's visits to his father's apartment to discuss business problems differ from Jacob coming to Isaac for the latter's blessing.

A BUSINESS FOR THE FAMILY

There can be no doubt that Charles Kurz realized his desire to have a business in which family members could find steady employment. Currently active in Keystone Shipping Company are his two sons, Adolph and Karl; three grandsons, Charles II, Donald, and Robert; and his nephew, Joseph E. Heidt, who is Assistant Manager, Operations for Agencies. Nephew Harry C. (Bud) Bennett, who first was employed in 1932, recently retired as President of Chas. Kurz Co., where great-nephew, David Bennett, was also employed for several years.

Three other family members whose employment for the Kurz organization spanned many decades were Charles's half-brother, Joseph C. Kall, Vice President, Operations, and President, Chas. Kurz Co., brother-in-law, Peter Heidt (Christina's husband), Port Steward; and, as previously mentioned, his brother Gus, who, except for a brief period when he left to enter the trucking business, worked with Charles from the time he was a teenager and became Director of Purchasing. All three remained with Keystone until their retirement.

Motivated by the memories of his own impoverished boyhood, Charles also offered employment to numerous graduates of Girard College, Philadelphia's renowned boarding school endowed by Stephen Girard for the education of "poor white male orphans."[2]

---

[2]Employees who were graduates of Girard College included Harry P. Buckley, Eberhard Dieterle, Leslie Edwards, Joseph W. Foy, Wesley L. Hoffman, Albert Longo, Robert S. Lukens, and Charles H. Matthias.

Charles used his resources not only to provide employment for family members, but also to offer assistance whenever needed. Even when he was in his late eighties, for example, it was largely he who took responsibility for the care of his sister Lizzie and brother Gus when they were in poor health or needed nursing home care. Thus he assumed the responsibility, and earned the respect, of family patriarch.

Epilogue

THROUGH THE PANAMA CANAL

Recently I had the thrill of boarding a tanker as it silently rose in the Gatun locks near the Panama Canal entrance on the Atlantic side. On her smokestack the letters "C.K." were displayed in blue on a field of gold. This was the Keystone insignia, utilizing its founder's initials and the colors of the State of Pennsylvania. In the next eight hours I was to enjoy what Charles Kurz himself has never experienced, a transit of the Panama Canal aboard a Keystone tanker.

That morning my wife Elisabeth and I were met at our hotel in Panama City at 4:30 A.M. and then driven across the isthmus of Panama from the Pacific side to the Atlantic side. The road passed through a dense jungle, now a forest preserve. Our driver, José Perez, stopped the car and turned off the lights in the middle of the jungle to show us what utter darkness is. By 6 A.M. it was daylight, and we approached the Gatun locks, which raise ships 85 feet from the Atlantic Ocean to the level of the artificial lake created in the early 1900s by construction of a dam on the Chagres River, the largest earth dam ever built up to that time. The Chagres is the only river in the world to flow over the continental divide and into two oceans.

When I saw the operations buildings, the locomotives which pull the ships, and the enormous gates at the ends of each lock chamber, I was swept by a wave of nostalgia. Everything was just as I had remembered it from November 1938, when I accompanied my parents on their Caribbean cruise.

We watched the *Petersburg*'s[1] slow approach in the sea level portion of the canal. As she eased into the first of the three

---

[1] This was a different ship from the *Petersburg* mentioned in Chapter 15.

151

chambers at Gatun, we were told to follow a guard across the narrow walkway on top of the mighty gate at the forward end of the first chamber. To our left was the water in the second chamber, a modest drop-off of about 30 feet; to our right, a terrifying 60 foot plunge to sea level.

In its closed position, the gate consisted of two 65-foot leaves, which met in an obtuse angle halfway across the lock. The slippery walkway on top of the gates seemed at most 16 inches wide. I grasped the railing on each side and tried not to look down. A gap of several feet was evident between the handrails of the first leaf and those of its mate at their junction. But we had come this far, and I wasn't about to turn back. I held on to one railing of the first leaf with one hand as long as possible while reaching ahead to the railing of the second leaf. Elisabeth followed, and we were soon on top of the 60-foot wide center wall separating the paired locks. As our heartbeats returned to normal, we noticed that the gate behind the ship had closed, and the *Petersburg* was rising in the first chamber. By the time we descended a flight of stairs and walked several hundred feet along the concrete wall, the deck of the ship was almost up to the level where we were standing.

A gangplank was mobilized, and Elisabeth and I walked safely aboard. We were greeted by the chief mate and third mate and then escorted aft to the superstructure and up three flights to the bridge. From there we had a breathtaking view of the deck with hatches for its three rows of tanks and a maze of pipes, valves, winches, hoses, and even a spare propeller. A sign painted at the outer edge of the bridge informed us that we were 568 feet from the bow and 168 feet from the stern.

We learned from the ship's captain, Timothy Hayes, that the *Petersburg* was nineteen years old and had been built by Bethlehem Steel, originally as the *Sinclair Texas*, before being bought by Chas. Kurz & Co., Inc. She is 50,000 tons deadweight, which refers to her carrying capacity: cargo, fuel, supplies, and a crew of thirty-three. The *Petersburg* carries only about 15,000 tons less than the largest cargo ever to transit the canal. She has about 3-1/2 feet to spare on each side when going through the locks, each of which is 110 feet wide. (Ships with as little as one foot to spare on each side, such as the USS *New Jersey* and her sister ships, hold the record for width.)

The size of the *Petersburg*, sixth or seventh largest in the present Keystone fleet of twenty-six, necessitates that she have four Canal Commission pilots aboard. They are in command during the entire transit, somewhat to the captain's dismay. At critical times one is at the outer edge of the bridge on each side and one on the foredeck on each side near the bow. They communicate by walkie-talkie and transmit their instructions for the ship's speed and direction via the captain to the person at the helm.

In addition, while going through the locks, some eighteen Panamanian workers come aboard to man the tow lines. These cables connect the ship to locomotives on a track atop each wall of the locks. On each side two of the towing locomotives pull the ship forward while one in the rear acts to slow or stop the ship's motion.

The size of the *Petersburg* also necessitated that, once having passed through the Gatun locks and into the open waters of Gatun Lake, she sit at anchor for about an hour and a half, together with a group of other large vessels, until the time allocated for one-way southbound traffic in the Gaillard cut, the narrow eight-mile channel near the Pacific end of the canal where the principal excavation through the mountains took place.

Not far from the entrance to Gatun Lake, we passed a smaller tanker going in the opposite direction. Captain Hayes was quick to point out that she was the *Mobilgas*, a Chas. Kurz & Co., Inc. ship which together with her sister ships, the *Mobilfuel* and *Mobilpower*, was chartered to Mobil.

The two Kurz ships passed in Gatun Lake, much as Charles Kurz had planned for his two chartered steamers, the *Eureka* and the *Tampico*, to pass in the early days of the canal's operation. When that plan was frustrated by landslides, little did he dream that his tankers passing one another in the Panama Canal eventually would become commonplace events.

The *Petersburg* was in ballast on her way to a Costa Rican port to take on a cargo of oil brought from Alaska in tankers too large for the Panama Canal. She would then return fully loaded via the canal and the Gulf of Mexico to Houston, Texas. For ships awaiting their turn to transit the canal delays of two or three days are not uncommon. In the case of the *Petersburg*, such a delay would cause an unacceptable increase in the time for such short voyages. Hayes explained that he had made a reservation for the *Petersburg*, for which the fee was $8,000. If

153

19. Passing the SS *Mobilgas* in Gatun Lake, June 1982.

that seemed like a lot, the toll itself was staggering: $75,000 when fully loaded, $40,000 when in ballast.[2]

The *Petersburg* has two captains, who work in rotation, for each has a day of vacation for every day worked. That sounds like a lot. Indeed it is a far cry from the agreement negotiated with the unions by Charles Kurz's committee of tanker owners in 1934, which provided 14-day annual vacations for licensed officers. But when working, the captain works continuously— Saturdays, Sundays, holidays. Hayes described his work day as often 12–16 hours while at sea and nearly around the clock while in port.

Later that day, standing on the highest level of the super-structure, known as the flying bridge, Elisabeth and I marveled at the engineering feat of gouging the eight-mile Gaillard cut through a saddle in the mountains where the original elevation at the continental divide was 312 feet above sea level. Most of it was built by blasting and digging through solid rock. Although the cut is now 500 feet wide and amply supplied with lights along its banks, ships as large as the *Petersburg* are permitted through it only during daylight and at times of one-way traffic. Moreover, a tug followed us all the way through the cut, pre-sumably as a safety measure in the event of power failure on the ship.

On the east bank our attention was caught by a lone waterfall cascading over the steep rocks into the canal. This, I learned later, was more than a scenic attraction. It was artificially cre-ated by diverting the stream above to that area to prevent wide-spread spilling and erosion of the bank.

We reached the end of the cut by mid-afternoon. Elisabeth and I now stood on the bridge to watch the maneuvering re-quired to turn this gigantic vessel somewhat to starboard to be aligned with Pedro Miguel lock, the first step of the descent to the Pacific. The tug, which had passively followed our passage through the cut, now moved to our port bow. Perpendicular to the tanker's hull, the tug strained with full force to push the bow to starboard, but the big ship seemed reluctant to budge.

---

[2]The highest toll ever paid was $89,154 (by the Queen Elizabeth 2), ac-cording to a Panama Canal Information Office brochure dated April 1980. The lowest toll was 36 cents paid by Richard Halliburton for swimming the canal in 1928.

20. View of the deck of the SS *Petersburg*, negotiating the Gaillard cut, June 1982. Note sailboat motoring in opposite direction.

21. Author standing on flying bridge by smokestack of SS *Petersburg*, bearing the insignia "C.K.," June 1982.

We listened to the commands of the pilot on the starboard bridge. Under the force of the tug, together with the towing locomotives and the ship's own power, the *Petersburg* gradually glided into Pedro Miguel. While the water level fell, the pilots exchanged tall tales of the sea, rumors of alligators spotted the previous day in a creek we would soon pass, and the like.

We had observed the arrival of a new crew of Panamanian workers to assist with the passage through the descending locks. One by one the men had climbed up a rope ladder thrown over the side of the ship, just as we had seen the first crew go down from the deck to a waiting launch after our passage through the Gatun locks. Elisabeth and I fully expected to leave the ship by climbing down the side on the same device, affectionately dubbed "Jacob's ladder."

Soon the *Petersburg* emerged from the final set of locks, the Miraflores. All efforts to spot alligators were fruitless. As we steamed toward the Pacific, a launch came alongside that I assumed was to pick up the Panamanian crew, but a message reached the bridge that it was to pick up Elisabeth and me. To my amazement, though, the "Jacob's ladder" was still on deck. Over the side a portable flight of steps, known as an accommodation ladder, had been suspended instead, enabling us to walk down about a 40 degree incline toward the stern of the ship. At the bottom we stepped from the ladder onto the deck of the tiny launch, as the water swirled beneath us. The launch pulled away, and we looked back at the huge tanker as she was about to pass beneath the Pan American highway bridge and into the Pacific Ocean. We stepped off the launch in the port of Balboa to be met again by José Perez and returned to our hotel filled with the fascination of the day's events.

The experience of transit through the Panama Canal produced three deep and lingering impressions. First, the locks, built long before anyone had heard of computers, are still functioning smoothly raising and lowering ships far larger than their designers ever imagined. The second was the enormous task of carving a path through the mountains, resulting in the beauty of the Gaillard cut.

The third impression was of the person whose initials were on the *Petersburg* smokestack. That evening Elisabeth and I each wrote him a letter. I gave him the facts about the trip, while our feelings were better expressed by her:

22. SS *Petersburg* sailing cut of Panama Canal toward Pacific Ocean, June 1982.

Today was surely one of the most fabulous days of my life, being aboard one of the Keystone ships, going through the Panama Canal.

At one point I was looking down from the bridge of the *Petersburg*, down onto this behemoth of a ship, when I was struck with an overwhelming feeling of admiration for you, Dad. I thought of the little boy you were who helped his mother support the family, and how that little boy had become the head of a company with so many of these giant ships! And how you are responsible basically for so many people making a very good living for themselves and their families.

I wish you could have been there today. I will just never forget the impression the canal made on me, such an unbelievable engineering feat. Neither will I forget the hospitality of the captain and crew of the *Petersburg*, or Fernie's[3] care of us, and their charming driver José. But most of all I will always remember that moment on the bridge when my thoughts went out to you and your accomplishments.

---

[3]C. Fernie & Co., Inc., ship agency for Keystone in Panama.

Appendix A

Navy Department
Office of the Chief of Naval Operations
Washington 25, D. C.

Serial 1866P421

1 Nov. 1946

Mr. Charles Kurz
Keystone Shipping Company
1015 Chestnut Street
Philadelphia, Pennsylvania

Dear Mr. Kurz:

The indispensable services rendered to the U. S. Navy during the war by commercial tankers has been widely accorded well-merited acclaim. As a leading figure in the tanker industry you are deserving of recognition for your splendid personal contribution to the Nation's war effort.

Prior to the outbreak of the war you recognized the Navy's need for high-speed tankers. As President of the Keystone Tankship Corporation, in cooperation with the U.S. Maritime Commission and the Standard Oil Company of New Jersey, you contracted for the construction in 1938 of two 18,256 ton high-speed tankers. Subsequently your company contracted for five additional vessels of a similar type. After a period of operation by your company all of these ships were acquired by the U.S. Navy for operation as commissioned fleet oilers.

You successively organized and served as Chairman of the first Tanker Committee, the Committee of American Tankers and the Tanker Committee of the American Merchant Marine Institute. These committees, which represented the owners and operators of U. S. commercial tankers, served as advisory bodies to the U. S. Maritime Commission, the War Shipping Administration and the U. S. Navy on a multitude of matters concerning tanker construction and operation. The unremitting labors of these committees were largely responsible for the efficient utilization of the Nation's tanker tonnage.

Early in 1941, at the request of the Government, you established the Keystone Shipping Company for the operation of Government requisitioned tankers. During the war this company operated over fifty tankers for the United States Government. These ships operated in every theatre of war transporting liquid cargo, military personnel and deck cargo which included military airplanes, PT boats, landing craft and foodstuffs. Under your able direction your company established an enviable reputation for efficiency and dependability.

Throughout the war you were intimately concerned with all phases of the tanker industry from the design of the ships to the training of shipboard personnel. Your sound and expert advice was at all times freely available to your Government.

For your outstanding contribution to the winning of the war I wish to tender to you my personal thanks and those of the United States Navy.

Sincerely yours,

C. W. NIMITZ
Fleet Admiral, U. S. Navy

Appendix B

TESTIMONIAL OF ESTEEM
Presented To
CHARLES KURZ

WHEREAS, Charles Kurz, a senior member of this Board, has tendered his resignation as Chairman of The Tanker Committee of the American Merchant Marine Institute, effective December 4, 1964, and

WHEREAS, he has served continuously and with distinction as Chairman of the said Tanker Committee since its organization on October 8, 1942, and

WHEREAS, Mr. Kurz has rendered many years of outstanding peacetime service to the Merchant Marine of the United States, both as a member of this Board and as a private shipowner, and

WHEREAS, he has rendered equally dedicated service to the military security of the United States through such public-spirited efforts as helping design the first National Defense Tanker; operating a vast wartime tanker fleet for the account of the Government, and organizing the Voluntary Tanker Plan, and

WHEREAS, his firm of Charles Kurz and Company, a Member Company of the American Merchant Marine Institute, has in the past year observed the Fiftieth Anniversary of its founding; now, therefore, be it

RESOLVED, that the Board of Directors of the American Merchant Marine Institute place on record its high esteem and friendship for the said Charles Kurz, its profound gratitude for his services as Chairman of The Tanker Committee, and its pleasure that he will continue to serve as a member of this Board; and be it further

RESOLVED, that an engrossed copy of these resolutions be presented to the said Charles Kurz on behalf of this Board.

THE AMERICAN MERCHANT MARINE INSTITUTE
By Order of the Board of Directors

Parker S. Wise   Ralph E. Casey
Secretary   President

New York, New York—January 14, 1965

163

Appendix C

AMERICAN MERCHANT MARINE INSTITUTE, INC.
919 18th Street, N. W.
Washington 6, D. C.
296-4450

Alvin Shapiro
Vice President

Earle C. Clements
Washington Consultant

June 14, 1963

PERSONAL

Mr. Charles Kurz
President, Keystone Shipping Company
1000 Walnut Street
Philadelphia 7, Pennsylvania

Dear Charley:

What does one say by way of congratulating you on your birthday? If I were to put it in my own way, I would indicate that your literally thousands of friends, in which class I would like to consider myself, wish you well and good health in the years ahead.

I have always deemed it a pleasure knowing you, having found in these many years that you were kindly and generous, you never once indicated a lack of gentleness, and you possess a monumental appreciation for the dignity of other people. That you have always been kindly and understanding to me goes without saying.

Continue for a long time to come being just what you have been in the past.

With every best wish.

Sincerely,

Al

ALVIN SHAPIRO

J. V. C. MALCOLMSON
135 East 42nd Street
New York 17, N. Y.

June 20, 1963

My Dear Charles,

I was invited and had hoped to attend your affair at the White House, but unfortunately I will be in Europe at that time.

You will realize that I speak for all your friends in Texaco when I say how delighted we were to learn that this honour was being conferred upon you and may we add how much we think you deserve it, more than anyone in the shipping industry.

Lord Geddes is coming in to see me in our London office on the morning of the 27th and I will make a point of telling him about your visiting with the Vice President of the U.S.A.

Please accept my good wishes and warm regards.

Jim Malcolmson

J. D. ROGERS
77 West 56th Street
Apt. 17B
New York 19, N. Y.

June 10, 1963

Dear Charley:

No one greeted with greater pleasure than I the announcement of your selection as Maritime Man of the Year by the Robert L. Hague Post of the American Legion. Recognition of your great contributions to the progress of the American Merchant Marine is long overdue. It would be difficult indeed to adequately measure the value of your achievements. Probably only those of us who worked with you and for you on industry problems are fully aware of the time & effort you devoted to solving the many problems with which we were faced over a long span of years.

More important, however, was the inspiration you gave to your associates publicly & privately. Your many kindnesses over the

165

years will always remain among my fondest memories. Your kind letter of last December containing good wishes on my retirement exemplifies your thoughtfulness and has been included prominently in my book of souvenirs.

It is my earnest hope that I can be present when you receive the Man of the Year Award. Heartiest congratulations and all good wishes for the future.

Sincerely,
John Rogers

Appendix D

OAK LANE PRESBYTERIAN CHURCH
North Eleventh Street at Oak Lane
Philadelphia 26, Pennsylvania

Richard S. Armstrong, Minister
6635 N. Eleventh Street (26)

September 21, 1963

Dear Mr. Kurz:

A year has passed—a year that began with the sadness of bereavement, and now ends with the sadness of memories made
vivid by this anniversary.

And yet it has been a triumphant year for you, a year in which
you have discovered, as only one who has known such grief can
discover, the reality of God's love. You have known the sus-
taining power of His Spirit and the peace of His abiding presence. You have learned as never before the comfort and strength
which He alone can provide.

It is only with the hindsight of faith that we are able to say
with Paul that in everything God works together for good with
those who love Him. This is the gift of faith, a gift which suf-
fering and sorrow seem to make us the more ready to receive.

I pray this day may be for you not just a time for tears but
a time for gratitude and even joy in the knowledge that faith,
hope and love abide, and nothing can separate us from the love
of God, which is in Christ Jesus our Lord.

Faithfully yours,

Dick Armstrong

ACKNOWLEDGEMENTS

Friends and relatives too numerous to name have provided bits of information and helped with background research pertaining to events recorded in this book. I especially wish to thank my brothers, Adolph and Karl Kurz, my stepmother, Anne Kurz, and my father's secretary, Catherine Grady, for their valuable assistance gathering information; my friend, John Moynihan, for his research; the ministers of St. Mark's United Church of Christ and Oak Lane Presbyterian Church, Thomas Souders and David Thompson, respectively, for delving into church records for answers to my queries; Janet Mayer and Carolyn Mealing for their expert typing; my cousin, Evelyn Breuninger Peck, for preparing the jacket illustration; and my wife, Elisabeth, for her consistent encouragement.

Sheila Segal provided valuable editorial assistance.

Most of all I appreciate my father's willingness to make his files available to me, to spend countless hours recounting the stories and answering my questions, and finally reviewing and suggesting improvements for the manuscript.

168